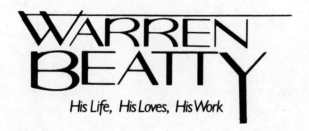

WARREN BEATTY

His Life, His Loves, His Work

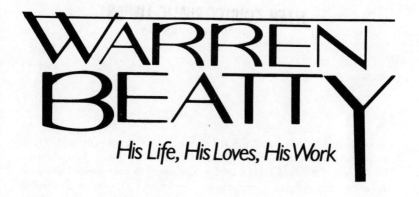

WARREN BEATTY

His Life, His Loves, His Work

SUZANNE MUNSHOWER

ST. MARTIN'S PRESS ● NEW YORK

Design by Lee Wade

Library of Congress Cataloging in Publication Data

Munshower, Suzanne.
    Warren Beatty—his life, his loves, his work.

    Includes index.
    1. Beatty, Warren, 1937– . 2. Moving-picture actors and actresses—United States—Biography.
I. Title.
PN2287.B394M79   1983   791.43′028′0924 [B]   83-9693
ISBN 0-312-85622-9

First Edition
10 9 8 7 6 5 4 3 2 1

7047791

CONTENTS

A section of photographs follows page 98.

ACKNOWLEDGMENTS

The author wishes to thank the many people who have been of great assistance, especially Marsha Daly, Sanford Schwarz, *Movie Mirror* magazine, the staff of the New York Public Library and the Billy Rose Theater Collection at Lincoln Center, Rona Barrett, Marvene Jones, Frank Edwards, Cyndi Wood, Bill Royce, Roberta Lawrence, Connie Berman, and the staff of the Academy of Motion Picture Arts and Sciences Archives.

WARREN BEATTY

His Life, His Loves, His Work

1

THE MYSTERIOUS
MR. BEATTY

In speaking of his friend Warren Beatty in 1978, writer Robert Towne made an astute comment. "People say you don't learn from success but from your failures," he noted. "Warren learns from success."

The culmination of the education of Warren Beatty thus far is the 1981 Academy Award for Best Director. For the man who had spent a full ten years of his life obsessed with bringing the story of journalist John Reed to the screen, the Oscar for *Reds* celebrated much more than his hard-won achievement as a director, as a force behind the cameras as well as in front of them. His win signaled a psychological victory as well. During his entire career in Hollywood, Beatty had determined to go his way and call his own shots. That gold statuette was the final proof of his wisdom, the ultimate confirmation that the independent path he'd blazed through the film industry had been a road to success.

The risk Beatty, and Paramount Pictures, took with the 3½-hour film was enormous. With a budget estimated at anywhere between $33.5 and $50 million and a subject popularly considered unpalatable, *Reds* appeared likely to fulfill the doomsayers' predictions and become yet another show business fiasco on the monumental scale of Michael Cimino's *Heaven's Gate*.

There was, of course, no happy ending for John Reed, the American who recounted the tumultuous days of the Russian Revolution in *Ten Days That Shook the World*, but the outcome of Beatty's involvement with Reed's life has been felicitous. He achieved a movie that has everything—politics, romance, commitment, scenery, grandeur—to guarantee its acceptance as a lasting work of art, a film that prompted reviewer David Israel to state that ". . . not since *The Godfather* has a film that aspired to such greatness achieved such greatness."

If, with *Reds*, Warren has accomplished the seemingly impossible task of making the Bolsheviks accessible to the masses, he has also, at age forty-six, managed to remain an enigma on a personal level. It's been twenty-two years since he first dazzled movie audiences as one of the star-crossed lovers in *Splendor in the Grass* (winning not only immediate stardom but co-star Natalie Wood as well), yet, to his friends as well as his fans, he's still a mystery in many ways. He delights in being quixotic and unfathomable, and his unpredictable behavior outdistances every other facet of his personality. Unlike so many other stars, whose whims and habits become as familiar to us as our own, Warren remains aloof, a quality that continues to challenge and fascinate others. Small wonder talk show host Dick Cavett recently asked guest Jerzy Kosinski, a peevish tinge coloring his words, "Why does he pronounce it *Beety* sometimes and *Batey* others?" Warren once told a reporter the correct pronunciation was "Badey"; still, pronounce it as you may, where Warren is concerned, there are no glib answers.

Over the years, he himself has made occasional attempts to define his own indefinability. "The only thing that is dangerous," he told one interviewer, "is boredom. I want to get out and do things that are different—not sit around and dwell on my own excrement."

He *has* done things that are different, and he's kept on the go so assiduously in his escape from ennui that *Bonnie and Clyde* director and close friend, Arthur Penn, once described him as "a very rich migrant worker."

Even the onset of middle age has served as a spur to this archetypal overachiever. Never one to sit back and rest on his laurels—the scarcity of motion pictures to his credit is the result of discernment, not laziness—Beatty is already hard at work putting together his next independent project, a film biography of Howard Hughes. He has not settled into his house on Mulholland Drive overlooking Los Angeles, not married Diane Keaton, not quit the entertainment business for the equally entertaining if more conservative field of politics. The grueling pace he has set for himself ever since he was a struggling youngster looking for a break in New York City has not slackened. Nor does it show signs of doing so. The man who has described what he calls the "best situations" as those where things got rough and he had to struggle continues to live for the struggle. To Warren Beatty, satisfaction isn't an end in itself. It's a prod, an impetus to seek out a greater challenge.

In 1975, five years before he began filming *Reds*, Warren revealed, "A hero like Reed appeals to me because he really gave himself to a great struggle, then got totally sapped by its bureaucracy and died. There was something a little bit ridiculous about him. I try not to ignore my own ridiculousness. Those old-fashioned heroes are embarrassing. Besides, I think I'm as noble as any of them."

One man who understands Warren's deep-rooted desire to be a new breed of American hero is writer Jerzy Kosinski, author of *The Painted Bird*, *Being There*, and *Pinball*, and, because of Beatty, an actor in *Reds*. Kosinski, a member of the Hugh Hefner crowd Beatty often pals around with, described his friend's rapport with the spirit of John Reed in a discussion with writer Aaron Latham.

"In Hollywood, which is a company town," Kosinski explained, "Warren has been a nonthreatened, very successful achiever. And so was John Reed in the company town of America until he committed himself to something that could have brought him down. What could Warren possibly do in the company town of Hollywood that would be revolutionary, truly qualitatively different from what Brando or Reynolds has done? Warren looked for a big subject, just as John Reed also looked for something big to report for the *Masses*. And so one day, Warren came across the story of John Reed—and he saw himself as John Reed. The project of making a movie about John Reed became what going to Russia was for Reed. It would affect his life."

To how great an extent the making of *Reds* has affected Beatty's life is something that remains to be seen. Though a general critical success, the film has not been an economic coup, not simply because of its extravagant budget, but also because its Oscar-winning director was unwilling to promote it as personally as some of the money men might have wished.

Still, as Robert Towne commented, Warren Beatty learns from success, and the lessons he's been taught by the success—and, most probably, the shortcomings—of *Reds* will be evident when his Howard Hughes bio-pic is wrapped and released.

In the meantime, Warren Beatty the actor continues to be a hot property, sought after for innumerable roles including the title role in the film version of Peter S. Feibleman's best-selling novel, *Charlie Boy*. Interestingly enough, Warren, who would actually be a better choice for the role of Joshua Moment, the strikingly handsome but extremely introverted physician whose life reaches an epiphany during a hurricane that occurs while he is attending a medical convention in New Orleans, is currently more interested in portraying the psychotic young killer whose tortured life becomes intertwined with the doctor's. But then, for Warren Beatty, the easy choice, the logical choice, the sensible choice, has never necessarily been the correct one.

This has held true for his entire life. Even as a high school senior back home in Virginia, he thought nothing of turning down one football scholarship after another to study acting instead, just as he later turned down one coveted film role after another with no regrets, just as he has resolutely shied away from marriage to some of the most marriageable women in the world.

Beatty's success with the opposite sex long ago passed from the stage of gossip to the pinnacle of legend. Among the women in his life he can count Natalie Wood, Leslie Caron, Julie Christie, Mary Tyler Moore, Michelle Phillips, Dayle Haddon, Maya Plisetskaya, Joan Collins, Britt Ekland, Joni Mitchell, Liv Ullmann, Carly Simon, Diane Keaton, and legions of women less well known but equally comely.

More than once, marriage seemed imminent, and Joan Collins even went so far as to announce their engagement. Still, as he approaches the half century mark, Warren Beatty remains that most desirable and enigmatic of men, the confirmed yet ardently heterosexual bachelor. So multitudinous are the stories of Warren's feminine conquests that Woody Allen (who, of course, was Diane Keaton's lover in her pre-Beatty days), when asked what he'd like to come back as in another life, quipped, "Warren Beatty's fingertips."

Women have always been a passion, but not to the degree that less romantic considerations haven't pushed them into the background. When Warren's busy on the campaign trail, as he was when he went into voluntary temporary retirement to work in the McGovern campaign, or when he's making a movie, the woman in his life has to settle for whatever time is left over. And with sixteen-to eighteen-hour workdays as the norm when he's busy on a project, there's not much time.

What makes a man so single-minded in the pursuit of success—success on his own terms—as Warren Beatty? The same balance of personal attributes that combine to make him so devastating to women and so acceptable to men. Beatty is a maverick in the true sense of the word, a man who has never stopped believing in his own values and principles, a man who doesn't buckle to public pressure where his life or his work is concerned. He is one of those rare human beings whose life, no matter how spontaneous it might appear on the surface, has never been a tale of impetuosity. On the contrary, his life has been a series of carefully mapped strategies and cautious decisions. And the rewards he's now garnering as a result of his precision planning are the very ones he's been steering himself toward since childhood.

2

A BOOKWORM
SHEDS HIS COCOON

In his notebooks, F. Scott Fitzgerald described a fictional character as "one of those men who come in a door and make any woman with them look guilty." Though the description fits Warren Beatty like a Savile Row suit, he didn't spring full grown from a Jazz Age novel. On the contrary, his childhood was more prosaic than dramatic.

Henry Warren Beaty was born March 31, 1937 in Richmond, Virginia, an area redolent of southern values and rich in atmosphere. His mother, the former Kathlyn MacLaine, was a schoolteacher who had taught acting in Nova Scotia, Maryland, and West Virginia; her marked interest in the dramatic arts would affect both her children. His father, Ira O. Beaty, now a realtor, was an educator who rose to be superintendent of Richmond High School.

Shortly after their son's birth, the Beatys moved to Arlington, Virginia, where both Warren and his sister Shirley attended school. Today, neither sibling speaks openly about their parents or childhoods, though Shirley MacLaine, in her autobiography, *Don't Fall Off the Mountain*, has portrayed her father as a strictly conventional man who preferred to keep everything on an intellectual rather than an emotional level.

That his father could be unapproachable at times is attested to by Warren's own comments. "My childhood was very strongly and positively affected by women," he's said. "My mother, my sister, my aunts, my great-aunts, cousins, all of whom were women—and I was fortunately not smothered by them. I trust women, generally speaking, more than I trust men."

MacLaine describes the Beatys' home as conventional and pristine, the typical residence of a striving middle-class family concerned with appearances and keeping up with the Joneses, filled with antiques and reproductions. Both Warren and Shirley grew into adults who couldn't care less about the material things of the world, who embrace causes but never possessions. Warren, in fact, has always taken a maverick pride in his lack of material acquisitions. A millionaire many times over, he responded to the question of whether he'd ever considered chucking it all and living in a shack by insisting, "I could do that. Until now, I've never owned anything during the fifteen years I've been a movie actor; I don't acquire things. I still don't live a life that I'd have trouble abandoning, even if I lost all my money."

Today, though he owns a house and a car—belongings he spurned until well into his thirties—Beatty still prefers to travel light, unencumbered by either tangible possessions or commitments.

Not that the children's lives were stark and uneventful. Mr. and Mrs. Beaty, though conformists, were far from dull, and both had a lively interest in the arts.

"Whatever real interest I had in movies and the theater came from my parents," Warren has admitted. "Both my mother and father were active creatively. She directed plays [his grandmother had been a teacher of elocution], he played the violin, and they were determined that Shirley and I would be disciplined in some means of self-expression.

"I never thought I would be an actor. I watched my mother direct, my father play the violin, and Shirley dance. I played the piano; maybe I just waited to spring. But no thought of getting up to perform. I was interested in the theater as a place to control, to manipulate."

Warren was, and still is, a talented piano player. Even as a child, he would work out his problems at the piano, running his fingers over the keys as he mused. Later, he put this musical talent to practical use, playing cocktail piano in New York as an aspiring actor and even getting a role as an ivory-tickling extra on a segment of daytime television's "Love of Life."

According to Shirley, the elder Beatys' love of performing had both a positive and a negative effect on their children. "Dad had this southern talent of commanding attention in any room with his storytelling," she reminisces. "Mom would react to him in an intense way. Though not social or gregarious, they were like a vaudeville team at home, and Warren and I would sit there and watch. It made us both rather shy, and one of our quests in life has been to overcome that shyness with self-expression."

It's likely that Warren's reluctance to step into the limelight was the result of shyness and insecurity rather than lack of interest. In his way, he pursued dramatic interests as an adolescent, miming to Al Jolson records in the privacy of the basement and memorizing the entire collected works of playwright Eugene O'Neill.

The youngster with the childhood nickname of "Little Henry" bore a strong resemblance to the comic strip character of the same name. Several years ago, as a guest on "The Pat Collins Show," Warren was surprised when his hostess flashed an old picture of Warren and Shirley, aged five and eight, respectively, on the screen. The snapshot, from his sister's private photograph collection, left Beatty bemused. "You shouldn't show me a picture like that on the air," he lightly chided Collins. "I have to sit and stare at it."

The snapshot revealed an elfin little boy clad in a cap and poplin jacket, looking straight into the camera with a shy, wistful smile, the adult's exceedingly handsome looks already evident. As his sister remembers, "When I was three, I used to dandle Warren on my knee, and even then I knew he was prettier than me."

He was known as "the Kid" in those days, a nickname still used by his sister and close friends. In those days, brother and sister were close, and there's no question that young Warren was infected by his older sister's streak of derring-do and tomboyishness. Shirley, though she played the model child on the home front, liked to raise Cain and make mischief when her folks weren't around. For the offspring of such southern propriety, harmless pranks like turning over garbage cans and ringing doorbells before dashing away seemed the height of deviltry.

The actor has never dropped his reticence about his family and childhood, but he's staunch in insisting any rumors of dissent and distance aren't true, stating that he continues to telephone his parents at least once a week. And he says it's totally untrue that there was ever any unpleasantness between his sister and himself after both had attained prominence in the entertainment field. They never reconciled their differences, according to Warren, simply because those differences were never serious.

"I'm still old fashioned enough to believe in maternal, paternal, and fraternal affection," he affirmed in 1970. "In other words, I love my mother, father, and sister very much. Shirley and I have our differences, but we respect each other and get along very well. It used to bug me when the press kept trying to stir up trouble between us. The so-called estrangement was reported several years ago when a big news magazine was preparing a Shirley MacLaine cover story. I was new to Hollywood, with only one movie under my belt, when a reporter called me on the telephone and wanted me to start talking about her.

"I said I didn't know what kind of thing they wanted to write about, and that I'd better not say anything until I knew more about what they were getting at. So the article came out and it said I refused even to discuss my sister and that I hung up on them. . . ."

According to Beatty, his sister was out of Los Angeles when the story broke. When she finally called him to ask about his behavior, he said she "understood completely" why he hadn't cooperated with the interviewer. But this, according to Beatty, is the basis of any and all reports of problems between the two. Maybe so, but that doesn't explain why Shirley told a different reporter in 1962, "I only know what I read in the papers about Warren. We rarely see each other any more. I've tried to reach out to him, but he just doesn't seem to want to communicate with me." Nor does it explain Shirley's appearing to take pleasure at the Academy Awards two years ago, when she publicly made jokes about her brother's reputation as a Don Juan as the cameras focused on an obviously disconcerted Warren with a blushing Diane Keaton by his side.

It's only natural that competition would take root in the Beaty household, where both academic excellence and artistic ability were expected to be the rule and not the exception.

Shirley, as the elder, found it easier to develop socially, and her dance lessons taught her to search out an audience early in life. Her brother was a late bloomer in the field of social graces. Warren's bedroom had a big closet with a window in it, and by this window he would sit in solitary study, reading books rather than joining in games. Intellectual pursuits were as important to the child as they now are to the man—until outside forces stepped in and pried him from his literary sanctum.

"I remember—I must have been thirteen—when one of my teachers said something to me about it not being quite fair for me to have a certain attitude because I was the best athlete in school," he recalls, "and I was stunned because the years before that, I had always been chided for being nonathletic. I played football, baseball, track every year, one after another. Football became a very important part of my life, a very important part."

The teacher set a challenge, and Warren discovered a trait hidden in his psyche that was to become a driving force: He liked challenges, and liked struggling to overcome obstacles. Not only was he going to become an athlete, he was going to become the best athlete.

His newfound enthusiasm for sports changed Warren's life in several ways. Not only did he put aside his books and turn athlete, he also discovered school popularity. He finished his school years not in the bedroom closet of the house on Arlington's Dominion Hill, but on the playing field and in the midst of other activities. By the time he graduated from Washington and Lee High School, the former bookworm had been offered ten college football scholarships and was popular with his classmates.

Warren's decision to study acting at Northwestern University in Evanston, Illinois, where the famed Alvina Krause has been credited with starting the careers of such diverse talents as Charlton Heston, Patricia Neal, Paula Prentiss, and Ann-Margret, could not have failed to dismay his father. The dedicated educator who had taught his son to read at age four had already been disappointed when his daughter left home to pursue a career as a dancer, and he'd even tried to talk her out of it, stressing that it is often better not to take a risk than to end up being second best. But Warren knew what he wanted, and what he wanted was to enroll at Northwestern's School of Speech, even though he was leaving himself open to the option of attending law school after he graduated.

What made the six-foot-one, 205-pound center (his weight dropped to 170 in his early acting days and now hovers around 175) turn his back on the sport that was the nucleus of his high school career? "I was sick of it," he admitted as a young actor. "It was a drag. Some things you want to do. . . . Some things you do to prove something. . . . Maybe it has to do with at a certain age in high school you want to prove you're a man."

He also admitted he didn't think he could ever have had a future in football. "I developed into a fair player for a period of about a year," he told Hedda Hopper, "but I never could have been as successful in college football as they seem to think I would. I didn't enjoy it that much. The important thing is doing what you enjoy, not because you get a reaction from others."

And so he set off to study acting, entering Northwestern in September 1955.

The School of Speech at Northwestern is housed in an old ivy-covered brick building in the center of campus, and it's around this building that the life of the drama majors has always centered. However, as a prestigious liberal arts college, Northwestern has never shirked giving its students a well-rounded liberal arts education. The freshman at Northwestern is allowed to pursue his major only in proportion to his general studies. It is a university, not an acting school, and while the speech courses offered at freshman level are varied and professional, a student cannot choose to specialize at the cost of a liberal education.

Warren stayed for a year, finding the school's approach to an acting career "slovenly, lackadaisical." He did not go out for sports, and the general course load of a full-time college student left little spare time for extracurricular dramatics.

Warren left for summer vacation, and he never went back. "I didn't make a decision, like this year I am going to quit and go out and do something," he confesses. "Things just sort of drifted out, and I thought, it's pointless to go back to school because it isn't what I want to do. I came to New York."

Shirley had made her own pilgrimage to Manhattan long before, heading for the city as soon as she graduated from high school. But rashness was always part of her makeup, and had never been a factor in Warren's decision-making processes. "I was always the outgoing one," she herself says. "Even as a child, Warren always wanted to wallow in the nuances of every situation."

That summer, the nuances consisted of measuring the parameters of his own future against the accomplishments Shirley could already claim. If he returned to school, he faced three more years of studying to get a degree that would promise no success out in the real world where acting was concerned. On the other hand, his sister, who had dared to strike out on her own, had already made it. Her success story was as romantic as Cinderella's with stardom striking like lightning when she was plucked from the chorus to substitute for Carol Haney when the star of *Pajama Game* injured her leg.

And so Warren decided that he, too, would forgo college and try his luck in New York in 1956, even though it meant admitting that he no longer considered the possibility of law studies. And, according to him, his parents accepted his decision. "They supported me in whatever I needed," he says. "I had my family's approval, I think, pretty much every turn I took. I think they had some amount of parental caution and skepticism about the theater. And I'm sure that would have increased had a few years gone by and nothing happened."

Beatty's parents have certainly supported him in one area over the years—by steadfastly refusing to talk to the press. Nor have they been in evidence in Los Angeles or New York at any of the many public functions attended by their famous son. They have kept to themselves back home in Virginia, the mother and father of two of the best-known entertainers in the world.

And they have watched as both their children shunned the strict monogamy they embraced. Shirley's lengthy marriage to producer Steve Parker was unconventional to say the least, with Parker (and for a majority of the time the couple's daughter Stephanie [Sachi] as well) living in his adopted country of Japan while Shirley remained in Hollywood. Since their official separation in 1976 and subsequent divorce, Shirley, who vigorously supports women's rights, has been linked with various men, but she hasn't appeared even slightly interested in marrying a second time.

"Neither of us would have a conventional marriage because of the intensity of the marriage we witnessed every day as children," Shirley has stated in an attempt to explain her and Warren's iconoclasm. "We need more breathing room in our lives. I can't imagine Warren with children. When he first met my daughter, he examined her quietly as though she were just a specimen of human life instead of his niece."

Warren, paradoxically, has shown a great deal of concern and warmth toward the offspring of several of his most serious romantic interests, notably Leslie Caron's son and daughter and Michelle Phillips' little girl, China. And he denies that he's not family oriented, chalking it up, as he does so much of the criticism aimed toward him, to false impressions.

"I threaten people," he says. "To some men, I seem to be what they would secretly like to be or are afraid of being. To some women, I am that fantasy figure, that object of desire and/or fear. But none of it is me! People seem to find my way of life, as they supposedly know it, to be dangerous. The family as we have known it has changed drastically. It has disintegrated to a large extent. People worry about this. Can they survive without the support of the family? They think I have. But that is not true. I *have* family. In my own way, I am very much a family man."

That way has included keeping the rest of the family out of the limelight, perhaps out of respect for their privacy as much as a careful guarding of his own.

And if Warren Beatty appears to be a man without a childhood, a man who sprang into prominence full grown, isn't that image solely the result of his own machinations? He's a long way from Arlington, and one can only suppose he has been ever since those days when he was a introverted bookworm, living in other places and as other people through the magical world of reading. He was eager to leave the things of his childhood behind. And he took his first determined step in that direction when he headed to New York, leaving Henry Warren Beaty far behind. Adding a "t" to his surname, he became Warren Beatty: Actor.

3

"THE KID"
ON HIS OWN

Those early years in New York constitute the single period of real material struggle in Beatty's life. Though he often presents himself as someone who just fell into acting, it's clear that he had his sights set on a career in the theater from the time he graduated from high school. Or even earlier. But now the youngster who'd once imitated Charles Boyer and Milton Berle as a child was out in the world, not in the basement of the family home. And success didn't come easily.

It was a difficult period for the young college dropout, but an educational and a broadening one as well. His parents, supportive though they may have been, weren't ecstatic at the second of their two children taking up what they considered a "way-out" profession. After all, in their household, dramatics were regarded as a pleasant avocation and not a potential career. But Warren's resolve was unbreakable.

He had already had one "professional" job in the theater, when, at seventeen, he'd worked as the official rat catcher at the National Theater in Washington, D.C., a job he'd been given after hanging around backstage asking if there wasn't something a willing and able teenager might do.

As luck would have it, a revival of *The Skin of Our Teeth*, with Helen Hayes in the lead, was opening, and earlier, there had been a bizarre incident at the theater, when a rat entered the building from the alleyway and bit an actor. The result was that Actors' Equity was pressuring the management to hire someone to eliminate the hazard and protect cast members.

And so Warren Beatty found his first job in the theater, though he was, in fact, literally outside the theater itself, standing in the alley on patrol to keep the rats out.

In Manhattan, things did not, at first, go much better. He lived in a grim $24-a-month furnished room on West 68th Street; in those pre-Lincoln Center days, the neighborhood was a rundown area of tenement rows, and his digs were a far cry from the succession of hotel rooms he would begin occupying when he found success.

"It was a junk heap," he told Tommy Thompson years later. "I mean a real junk heap because a junkie had lived there before. And the smell was still there."

Beatty's life in the big city wasn't much different from the lives of other hopeful young thespians then and now. He lived as frugally as possible, eating countless peanut butter sandwiches and spending the better part of his hard-earned money on acting lessons, though he still won't admit he intended to be an actor. He studied with the renowned Stella Adler, he says, because he was considering directing one day, but insists, "I never intended to be a movie star. If anything, I had vaguely intended to go into law and then politics. No one in his right mind sets out to be a movie star because it seems like a capricious gamble to take."

Obviously, Ira Beaty's advice to his daughter—that it was better not to try than to risk failure—had registered deeply with his son as well.

In the meantime, Beatty earned his keep by washing dishes, working as a sandhog on the third tube of the Lincoln Tunnel, and playing cocktail piano. Beatty, who jokes that he wasn't "any Carmen Cavallaro—just a half-baked piano player," played at Clavin's, a gin mill on East 58th Street no longer in existence, surely a more enjoyable way of supporting oneself than slogging away at a construction job or in a steamy restaurant kitchen. Music, especially jazz piano, has remained Beatty's second love next to acting, and he would later follow up his extra work at the keyboard in "Love of Life" by headlining (opposite Elizabeth Taylor) as a lounge pianist in George Stevens' *The Only Game in Town*.

He was also well on his way to establishing himself as a man about town, and among those he dated was a young actress named Diane Ladd (who would later marry and divorce one of his Hollywood contemporaries, Bruce Dern). Diane shared an apartment with three other young single women, one of whom, Rona Barrett, found the young man's aggressiveness, so alluring to Diane, a bit intimidating.

Too much work combined with too much play sapped the strength of "the Kid," and he wound up back home in Arlington recovering from a bout of hepatitis. But his misfortunes in New York didn't defeat him. Instead, as soon as he was well enough, he headed right back into the fray, determined to see things through.

His persistence paid off, for between 1957 and 1959 he began getting small roles on television and in stock productions. One of his first breaks came when he accompanied a friend to an audition, volunteering to play opposite him in his audition scene. The friend lost out, and Warren won the minor role.

On CBS, he was seen on "Studio One" and "Playhouse 90"; on NBC, he played the lead in Kraft Theater's "The Curly-Headed Kid." On stage, he did summer stock at the Gateway Theater on Long Island and winter stock at the North Jersey Playhouse in Fort Lee, playing a variety of roles that broadened his versatility as an actor. He was twenty-one years old. If he had stayed in college, he would have been about to graduate with a Bachelor of Science degree in speech.

Instead, here he was, slowly establishing himself as an actor and learning his craft by playing one part after another in stock and on live television. Perhaps this is how his life might have gone on for another few years if fate hadn't intervened and seen to it that he was discovered. However, the "overnight success" wasn't exactly a neophyte. By the time he was plucked from obscurity to be thrust onto the Broadway stage in a major role, Warren had acted in approximately fifty productions.

His break came while he was appearing in a New Jersey stock production of Meyer Levin's *Compulsion*. He was spotted by director Joshua Logan, who was interested in the young unknown for the upcoming movie *Parrish*.

Beatty flew to California, where he screen-tested opposite another movie novice, Jane Fonda. Hollywood legend has it that their screen kiss was so sizzling they didn't hear the director yell "Cut!" but this seems unlikely, since both young thespians were already too ambitious to allow passion to interfere with their budding careers.

As it turned out, Warren didn't win a role in the turgid soap opera that was later made with Troy Donahue, another of the late fifties' "instant stars," in the title role. But his presence in California didn't go unnoticed. Three months after his screen test, MGM offered him a five-year contract at $400 a week.

Those were the days of contract players, a star-making system that spawned some of the most forgettable screen actors of our time as well as some of the most embittered talents. When a young actor signed his soul over to a major studio, it seemed to be the lucky break of a lifetime. But for many, it became little more than bondage, as their contracts required them to essay one mediocre role after another.

Not this twenty-two-year-old actor. Warren was already too certain of what he wanted and how he wanted to get it to let himself be caught in the gears of studio commercialism. When MGM decided their new player should appear in the film *Strike Heaven in the Face*, the young actor did more than balk at the title. He did what he was to do frequently in his career—he turned it down.

Turning down a first film role was unheard of in those days, but that mattered little to Warren. Borrowing money, he bought his way out of his contract and headed back to New York.

While in Hollywood, Beatty had been asked to read for William Inge's film *Splendor in the Grass* in New York, where the script's director, Elia Kazan, was currently working. Now, with his contractual obligations a thing of the past, Beatty flew back to Manhattan, only to learn that the film had been postponed.

But the news wasn't all bad. Playwright Inge had spotted the young man's talent, and he made sure Warren got the leading role in his new play, *A Loss of Roses*. It was here that Warren began gaining his "bad boy" reputation. He argued with both the show's director, Daniel Mann, and his famous co-star, Shirley Booth, about everything in the staging that didn't suit his fancy. His tyrannical behavior may have had its roots in insecurity—it had its results in Inge's taking Beatty's side against Mann whenever disagreements broke out, and in Shirley Booth's quitting the show before it opened.

Though the unpleasantness surrounding it was of his own making, the experience soured Beatty on the theater. He has never appeared on stage again.

A Loss of Roses was a large-scale failure, closing after just three weeks. But for Beatty, it was a personal victory. His own reviews were good; people were starting to take notice of what Britain's Kenneth Tynan, writing for *The New Yorker*, described as a face that was "sensual around the lips and pensive around the brow."

He had also made two very influential and important friends. William Inge became a staunch supporter who stuck up for his protégé in the face of some unflattering criticism then and later. "Warren is really kind of like a young colt who's out in a new green pasture," he said in defense of the actor after Warren had returned to Hollywood and gained a reputation as a difficult, bossy young know-it-all. "He's nervous about making a picture and it brings out a most self-protective quality.

"As a result, he's very reluctant to trust people in charge. He has the feeling he has to design the set, the costumes, the makeup, and sometimes you want to say, 'Oh, shut up and do your part.' But he's basically a very fine kid who will eventually learn a way of working with people."

The playwright died before the making of *Reds*. If he had lived longer, he might have been amused to watch Warren overseeing every single aspect of his production from the set to the costumes to the makeup, even to the morale of the extras. The "way of working with people" he finally discovered and settled upon was to produce, direct, co-write, and star in his own motion picture rather than relinquish control over any facet of the film's making.

Another who befriended Beatty was Elia Kazan, who was in complete agreement that Warren was perfect for *Splendor in the Grass*. "I liked Warren right away," recalls Kazan. "He was awkward in a way that was attractive. He was very, very ambitious. He had a lot of hunger as all the stars do when they are young."

The admiration between "Gadge" Kazan and Beatty is mutual, and Warren still refers to his first film director as his favorite director.

Kazan had already helped to create one matinee idol when he directed the young James Dean in *East of Eden*. Now he was pairing the late screen idol's *Rebel Without a Cause* co-star, Natalie Wood, with another pouting, sensual newcomer, sure that the chemistry between the two as the star-crossed young lovers in Inge's tragedy would give him another hit.

Warren was pleased at the chance to star in a movie at last, but he wasn't thrilled. He had been too selective and careful about his career to be easily thrilled. After all, *Splendor in the Grass* wasn't the first film he had been offered; it was the first he had accepted.

By the time he was twenty-two, the actor's certainty that he, and only he, knew what role, what co-star, which director were right for him was already firmly implanted. He was determined to call his own shots and never to allow anyone to treat him as an unimportant entity, no matter how his behavior might wreak havoc with his future.

"People spit all over actors," he said resentfully in 1961 when talking about his struggles as an unknown. "It's a shame the spitters are usually in the business."

He refused to curry favor with anyone, especially those he felt behaved insultingly. Once, when he had what promised to be a "sure" job, he was told to shine his shoes. Instead, he stood up and left, blowing all chances of getting the part. Another time, he was called to read for a role he badly wanted. But when the director, before Warren had a chance to begin reading, said, "All you young actors are mumblers," Warren thrust the script back at him and stormed out.

Defiant, yes. But also dedicated, ambitious, and motivated. From the start, there were no rash moves, no quicksilver decisions for the young man from Virginia whose favorite expression has always been "I'll think about it." He was taking carefully measured steps in the direction of the stardom he sought, and nothing—neither studio executives nor directors—was going to sway his own thoughtfully chosen path.

The young Beatty's actions and reactions were often chalked up to temperament and sheer orneriness. Certainly much of his behavior was born of youth's desire to shock and refusal to compromise. But a great deal of the actor's headstrong independence and unbendable will was the result of his vision and foresight. He was carefully molding his image and his career, already determined to control as much of any production as he could. He relied on no one's judgment, no one's expertise except his own, and the fact that he was an inexperienced greenhorn in the eyes of Hollywood's professionals didn't faze him. He weighed all options before he committed himself to anything, but once he was committed, he was indefatigable.

Time has not mellowed his resolve. "It would be nice," he confessed to Charles Champlin in 1975 when he was firmly established as both a star and a millionaire, "to be able to do everything I want to do and say everything I want to say, when I won't be carrying the responsibility of so many people and when all the accoutrements of making film are taken care of. I'm trying to get a little more relaxed with all that, but it ain't easy.

"There are a lot of things you'd like to do in film, but you have to be damned careful you do them right, because there aren't any second chances, not in film, no matter who you are."

Those were the words he lived by from the day he decided to

be an actor, and since there weren't going to be any second chances, he was going to do everything possible to do what he thought was right, regardless of what anybody else thought.

"What others criticize you for, cultivate: it is you." These words of French writer and playwright Jean Cocteau might have been written for young Warren Beatty. Instead of downplaying his drive toward total control, he came close to flaunting it, and the directors he worked with best were always those who would listen to, and often follow, his advice.

Warren's cultivation of his independence wasn't well received by Hollywood in general. Even before *Splendor in the Grass* was released, interviewers were giving Warren negative reviews: criticizing his brashness and lack of humility and implying that here was this year's flash in the pan. When the film opened, there was no rational basis for disparaging his performance, so they continued to concentrate on his attitude instead.

He has, of course, survived to have the last laugh, and it's that same know-it-all attitude that has made his success a lasting one. Warren Beatty's victory in Hollywood finally came when he took the reins of film production into his own hands and did what he'd wanted to do from the start—took responsibility for every phase of the making of a movie. But in 1959, that victory lay more than two decades in the future. For the next few years, Warren would find himself pigeonholed as an uncooperative, egotistical young actor who was most probably heading for a downfall.

4

NAT AND R.J.
AND JOAN AND WARREN

"To love oneself," Oscar Wilde once said, "is the beginning of a lifelong romance." This surely holds true for Warren Beatty, one of whose women friends remarked that the man was so in love with himself, it was contagious.

He'd gained a reputation as a ladies' man in Hollywood before his handsome, pouting visage had even flashed across the big screen, so it's no wonder that, for most of his long career as an actor, his romances have garnered more press coverage than his performances.

Warren hooked up with English actress Joan Collins when he was still an unknown actor, meeting her when he flew to California for his screen test before opening in New York in *A Loss of Roses*. Beatty had seen some stills of the green-eyed, raven-haired actress and decided he just had to see her. A friend suggested he see *The Big Country*, Joan's current movie release. "We had not met at this stage," Joan later reminisced, "and Warren went along to the film to decide whether he would like to meet me in person. Well, he was very disillusioned by what he saw. And he came away saying I was not so hot after all."

He may have been disillusioned by her acting abilities at the time, but he wasn't unimpressed when he finally saw her in the flesh. Warren had a date, Joan had a date, but they took one look at each other and one of the most heavily publicized romances of 1960 was born, with Warren calling her the next day and later gushing to Earl Wilson in a very un-Beattylike way, "She's got eyes that are big pools. When she's in the rain, she looks like a rain goddess. . . . She's got the kind of face that will get more beautiful the next fifteen or twenty years!"

More than twenty years have passed since Beatty said those words, which have proved to be prophetic. Joan Collins *is* more beautiful than she was in 1960. She was also the first of many famous and gorgeous actresses Warren Beatty didn't marry.

In 1960, the two were engaged, and Warren was so infatuated that when *Seven Thieves*, in which Joan played a stripper, came out, he insisted, "I'll be watching it seven or eight times a day," the first and last time Warren ever babbled like a schoolboy about his love life.

And what a love life it was! The newspapers and gossip columnists had a field day, understandably so. Joan Collins was a popular sex goddess, fifties style, with a tightly-packed 126 pounds on her five-foot-five frame, arranged in provocative 38-23½-37 proportions. And she played her role to the hilt, once reportedly wearing a dress so tight she had to be carried up a flight of stairs to make an appearance!

At her side, the handsome, tall, dark-haired actor with the sensitive, myopic blue eyes was sure to be noticed, and the fact that his girlfriend was already a star, with twenty-five starring roles to her credit, didn't hurt, either.

It wasn't just Joan's physical attibutes or movie experience that made her newsworthy. Her personal life had made headlines as well. In 1956, when women's liberation was pretty well unknown, Joan divorced Maxwell Reed, an unemployed British actor she'd married when she was nineteen and he was thirty-one. When they split up, he sued her for $1,200 a month alimony.

So unheard of was such behavior at the time that, at the trial, the divorce judge asked Joan if her husband was in some way incapacitated. Her reply was to the point: Maxwell was perfectly equipped to earn his own living. The court denied Reed's alimony request, with Joan, on the advice of her lawyers, agreeing to pay a flat $6,750 settlement he had requested. When the divorce was final, Joan said of the man she'd once described as "older, but mentally . . . years younger than me," simply, "I was silly and immature when I married him. I was crazy."

Nor did the ravishing Miss Collins make headlines only because of her legal woes. The gossip columnists had a field day when Lieutenant Rafael Trujillo, playboy son of the Dominican Republic's dictator, was enraptured by her charms. The younger Trujillo was a ladies' man who collected screen sirens as another man might collect stamps. He had already been linked with both Kim Novak and Zsa Zsa Gabor when he presented Joan with a $10,000 diamond bracelet as a token of his affections. But Joan, who at this time was declaring that "marriage is a trap," granted her suitor no special loyalties. She was fresh from a romance with Arthur Loew, Jr. (who later dated Natalie Wood) when she met Warren at that Hollywood party.

Warren was then living at the Chateau Marmont Hotel, an actors' hangout above Sunset Boulevard in West Hollywood, when he wasn't in New York. And not long after their meeting, Joan quickly forgot about escaping the bondage of marriage and announced she was engaged to the young, unproved actor.

Beatty, though open about his adoration of the British actress, refused to commit himself publicly to the possibility of an impending marriage, firmly closing discussions that strayed into queries regarding matrimony with a succinct, "I wouldn't dream of talking about that."

Shooting had just begun on *Splendor in the Grass* when Joan left the country to star in *Esther and the King* in Europe. When she left, she gave no sign that she and Warren were headed anywhere but for the altar.

But then, she hadn't reckoned on the chemistry between Warren and co-star Natalie Wood, either.

Natalie Wood at twenty-two was everything Warren wasn't. Born Natasha Gurdin, she had been groomed for show business since she was a toddler, making an impressive screen debut at the age of eight with Orson Welles in *Tomorrow Is Forever*.

So many child stars never manage to make a graceful transition from precocity to maturity on the screen, but Natalie's fragile beauty and undeniable talent kept her from joining the ranks of Deanna Durbin, Jane Withers, and Shirley Temple. She established herself as an adult actress of indisputed worth in 1955, when she sizzled onscreen with James Dean and Sal Mineo in *Rebel Without a Cause*, the now-classic story of mixed-up youth and misunderstanding parents.

Now, in *Splendor in the Grass*, she was filming another tale of rebellion and unhappy young love, playing opposite the actor many were already calling the "new" James Dean. The chemistry between the two was expected to light up the screen.

That the chemistry might prove explosive off the screen as well hadn't occurred to anyone. After all, Natalie, unlike Warren, was married, and had been for three years, to clean-cut actor Robert Wagner.

He called her "Nat," she called him "R.J." and it was impossible to open a fan magazine in those days without reading every detail of their perfect marriage—their salt-water swimming pool, their movie star mansion, their his and hers sports cars.

Their devotion was genuine, as was their vow never to be separated if they could help it. However, since the one film they made together—*All the Fine Young Cannibals*—landed at the box office with a resounding thud, they had no choice but to make other work commitments.

During the filming of *Splendor in the Grass*, Wagner made an effort to be present as often as possible, but often wasn't enough. Years later, after they had both divorced others and remarried, Natalie and Wagner admitted that the strain of their overpublicized, life-in-a-goldfish-bowl marriage had been getting to them for a long time before the marriage broke up. If Warren Beatty hadn't come along, it's a safe bet someone or something else would have.

But what came along *was* Warren Beatty, and by August 1960, the five-foot-two, ninety-eight pound actress was seen everywhere in the company of her magnetic young co-star.

In the meantime, Joan Collins was left in the lurch, telling whoever would listen that it had been *her* idea not to marry. "Everyone talked about our marriage except us," she insisted. "We're no longer engaged because I don't want to answer to a studio *or* a husband. I hate plans and I'm very fickle."

There was clearly no love lost between Collins and Wood from the start, since, several years earlier, when Collins was appearing on a television show with Wagner and he mentioned his forthcoming marriage to Natalie, she tartly snapped, "Lots of luck. You'll need it."

With Warren out of the picture, Joan went on to a romance with Robert Wagner in a classic change of partners. Now starring on TV's "Dynasty," Joan told all about her relationship with Beatty in her autobiography. In the book, originally published only in England after Collins returned a $100,000 advance to keep it out of America, she related such tidbits as, "He [Warren] was insatiable. Three, four, five times a day, every day, was not unusual for him, and he was also able to accept phone calls at the same time."

"I prefer not to talk about a divorce," Natalie pleaded after her split from Wagner was official. "And as for Warren, I don't want to talk about him, either. I have no plans whatever for being married again. I simply want to be the best actress I can possibly be. I guess my life has been molded by my environment, just as anyone's life has."

But there was no question that she was in love with Warren, who was omnipresent, both of them collapsing into giggles each time they assured reporters, "We're just friends!"

Warren by now had learned one of the lessons of fame, and he was immovable in his refusal to talk about his affair with Natalie. "I never have thought it was fair to talk about people I have a personal relationship with," he told Louella Parsons when she tried to dig beneath his reserve. "I figure if I have a blanket rule like this, then people know I won't talk about them. . . . The questions don't offend me. I just don't answer them. I've never thought I could keep my private life private and still be a movie actor. But I just don't talk about it."

At other times, though, Beatty was less polite about the prying into his personal life; he made no secret that the questions did offend him.

"I've given you too much of my time, much too much," he informed one reporter early in the 1960s. "All you're interested in is the neurotic side of me. You don't want to write about my work. You haven't asked me a single question about my ideas on acting, about the theater or anything I consider important. My childish ego is excited by the prospect of your writing a story about me, but all you're interested in is trivia."

It was, alas, the "trivia" that sold magazines, and his attitude served the negative purpose of focusing reporters on Warren's "childish ego" more than anything he thought or had done professionally.

Once or twice, he tried to open himself up to a journalist and discuss the prospects of a marriage between himself and the now available Miss Wood, but the inarticulateness Warren has always exhibited when put on the spot about personal relationships made his answers ambiguous. "I am confused about marriage," he told one reporter, while to another who asked if the actor and actress would marry, he simply murmured, "I don't know. We have a good time together, and we speak the same language—the language of motion pictures and of the theater." And that was as strong a statement of passion as he was willing to make.

Words weren't really needed, however; it was easy to see how enamored the screen lovers were of one another offscreen as well. And while Nat awaited her divorce decree from Wagner, the two made plans to co-star again, in the film version of *Sunday in New York*, a big hit on Broadway that year with a young unknown stage actor named Robert Redford in the lead. This was the beginning of a trend for Warren, who invariably shows great interest in scripts suitable for himself and his inamorata of the moment. In this case, as in many others that still lay in the future, the infatuation fizzled first, and in its wake plans for any mutual film commitment were scrambled.

Natalie showed up to receive her divorce decree attired in black from head to toe, looking tinier and more vulnerable than ever as she faced a future that didn't appear to include either of the men she had loved. "Everyone searches for happiness," she mused. "Most people search for what makes them happy. I guess I just haven't found it yet."

She did find it finally—with the man she had married when she was little more than child. In the years between their first and second marriages to each other, both Wood and Wagner grew up. By the time they'd both divorced their second marital partners and rediscovered each other, they no longer resembled the immature movie stars whose fairy-tale union had left no room for reality. Instead, they were seasoned performers who'd worked hard in the intervening years and had become "actors" rather than "stars," who had weathered bad relationships and another unsuccessful marriage apiece before finding each other again. Their remarriage was considered one of filmdom's happiest, revolving around their daughters (one from each remarriage and one of their own) and built on a foundation of privacy that brought a deeper satisfaction than they'd ever found in the plethora of publicity more than a decade earlier.

As for Warren, he had no time to brood over the end of the affair. He himself remarked, "It's a strange situation to suddenly be somebody. A year or so ago, I couldn't get a job in a film." *Splendor in the Grass* had changed all that. He had been, suddenly and irrevocably, discovered. At twenty-four, he found his name a household word, and never again would anonymity be his.

Sudden success and notoriety are difficult for even the most seasoned veteran to handle, and one has only to recollect the recent exorbitant demands and temper tantrums of some of our "overnight" television sensations to understand what a jolting effect such rapid renown can have on the young.

Beatty didn't wear the cloak of instant stardom lightly. From the moment he set foot in Hollywood, he began building a reputation as an enfant terrible, a cocky and arrogant egotist who could make life on a film set sheer hell for others more experienced than he.

Now he began pursuing better roles, other women, and having his own way whenever possible with a vengeance. His behavior was usually more newsworthy than his films, making people sit up and take notice of him. It was only years later that he came to grips with another result of his behavior. Many people refused to take Warren Beatty seriously.

5

"SUDDENLY YOU LOSE YOUR ANONYMITY. . . ."

The brash young star made good copy, with his piquant mixture of Lothario and spoiled brat. The sexual nature of his role in *Splendor in the Grass* was highlighted by the ever lengthening string of names linked with his, and when his romances didn't thrust him into the gossip columns, his sulky arrogance did.

A description of the actor as an angry young man in the September lst issue of *Time* magazine summed up Warren as others saw him in 1961:

> With a facial and vocal suggestion of Montgomery Clift and mannerisms of James Dean, he is the latest incumbent in the line of arrogant, attractive, hostile, moody, sensitive, self-conscious, bright, defensive, ambitious, stuttering, self-seeking and extremely talented actors who become myths before they are thirty.

Warren fed the myth by reacting in a typically quixotic way to the description. With righteous indignation, he protested, "I don't stutter. Obviously, the guy who wrote that doesn't know me." The remainder of the taunts and tributes didn't affect him at all.

Today, Beatty is a far cry from the petulant newcomer who, if not hellbent on offending everyone with whom he came in contact, made no effort to ingratiate himself. He remains a difficult, uncommunicative subject during an interview (Barbara Walters once named him the most difficult interview she'd ever done), but now his refusal to discuss anything but what he wants to discuss is covered by a veneer of politeness and concern.

Still, he continues to slough off the blame for his bad reputation of yesteryear. "It was worse when I was starting out in movies," he said not long ago regarding the humiliation of public life.
"The lot of the young actor or actress is particularly difficult. They
know that a certain amount of the fame they receive relates to their
youth and physical beauty, and it engenders a tremendous amount
of hostility in them. They also know what has happened to their
predecessors and what will happen to them. This goes for models,
too—anywhere a person is used essentially as a sex object."

The dehumanizing effects of fame, especially in the show business sphere, are unarguable. Beatty wasn't the first or the last star to
discover that the life of a celebrity wasn't all it was cracked up to be
or that the film business is simply that—a business. Like so many of
the disillusioned youngsters who have come after him, Warren
struck out at those he blamed for treating him as a thing rather than
as a person.

"More and more, you've got to put things in perspective," he
mused discontentedly in 1963. "Acting, show business. Let's say
you can go and do a movie and you have high hopes for it and
something goes wrong. If that's everything, you find yourself
unhappy.

"You think the business is an art form, and then you find
yourself all disillusioned, and that can be a shock. . . . And after a
while, the only thing that becomes important is to express yourself
and not to worry about what happens.

"I don't know how to assimilate the idea of being thrust out like
a *product*. Suddenly, you lose your anonymity, and once you do,
you can't get it back."

Describing himself as someone who has been "badly burned"
by interviews, Beatty nowadays talks to the press only when he's
promoting a film or political cause. And even then, he loathes the
experience. And he knows from experience that no matter what he
does or doesn't say the press and the public will draw their own
conclusions.

"I have never talked about my personal relationships—with

women, my sister, my parents—because these are important people to me," he admits. "I don't want to hurt them by discussing them in public. As for my love life, I can't control what others say about it. I know that movie actors are overrewarded in our society, and that the press has to cut people like me down to size. So they come up with all sorts of wild things. They make me into an insane eccentric with an incredible fear of losing my youth, who lives in a bomb shelter, who contemplates or is going through plastic surgery, who has devastating relationships with women. It goes through cycles. First they say women like me too much; then that women don't like me at all; then that they like me too much again. Somewhere along the way they say that I secretly like men—but then that men don't like me! I'm old, I'm young, I'm intelligent, I'm stupid. My tide goes in and out."

Establishing himself as a sex symbol so early certainly didn't help Warren as far as prying questions were concerned. Each time an interview was set up for him (and a young actor doesn't have much choice about meeting the press if he wants people to pay to see his movies), he'd be uncomfortably aware that he was letting himself in for an impossible situation. He wanted to talk about his craft and his artistic beliefs; they wanted to hear about his love life and his libido.

"You know that interviewing movie actors is usually a boring business," he told a reporter from the Providence *Journal-Bulletin* in 1975. "You've got to get the story written, and the actor is supposed to plug the picture. Usually, neither of you wants to do the thing.

"You can't talk only about the picture. That invalidates the whole thing—if you can verbalize it, then why did you bother to make the movie? So why do a disservice to the movie? After all, it's not my movie anymore. It exists on its own. At a certain point, it takes over from you and the people who were involved with it and takes off on its own. So the worst thing you can do about a movie is to talk about it too much, to intellectualize about it.

"So you end up talking about yourself. These interview situations force a person to tap all his narcissistic reserves.

"You can kill a movie just by turning up in magazines and newspapers and on talk shows until you make people sick of you. . . ."

Of course, Beatty's reserve and reluctance to talk about his personal life has had its own publicity value, engendering volumes of copy on the tantalizing subject "What's Warren Beatty really like?" Conjecture is oftentimes more seductive than fact.

But protest as he might that he's been "a victim of many writers," Beatty's early behavior paints him more as the victim of his own attitude. It was Beatty, and not the press, who argued with directors, threw a studio publicity photographer out of his dressing room for invading his privacy, made outrageous demands and insisted they be added to his contracts, and infuriated one director by taking longer with his makeup than the leading lady. And there was never any question about his being in a hurry to be a star. Even in a town so reeking with ambition as Hollywood, his lust for success assumed legendary proportions. When Beatty wanted something, he would go to enormous lengths to get it.

The lengths Warren went to in order to get his second movie role illustrate his determination and his refusal not to be deterred by a simple "no." He wanted to star in *The Roman Spring of Mrs. Stone*, and if he could do anything to guarantee his getting the role, he would.

Then, as he was on his way to the airport to catch a flight to London, he got the bad news: though both the leading lady, Vivien Leigh, and the director, Jose Quintero, had given their approval of Beatty's portraying the young Italian gigolo who captivates a wealthy older woman, final approval of the casting rested with writer Tennessee Williams and Williams was adamant that the gigolo be played by a bona fide Italian.

The determined stripling wasn't about to be rebuffed so casually. At the airport, he changed his reservation and caught a plane to

Puerto Rico, where the flamboyant author of *The Glass Menagerie* and *A Streetcar Named Desire* was vacationing.

Then, as Beatty himself recalls, ". . . I walked up to him in a gambling casino and began to talk to him in an Italian accent. In fact, I brought him a glass of milk on a tray, because I had been told that he had ulcers from his reviews of *Sweet Bird of Youth*.

"He fell on the floor and said, 'All right, all right. You've got the part.' I went to London."

The reviews of *The Roman Spring of Mrs. Stone* couldn't have helped Williams' ulcers much, especially as more than one critic found Beatty's flamboyant Italian accent laughable. Though the movie didn't add to Beatty's reputation as an actor, the rumors of an offscreen romance with the dazzling star of *Gone with the Wind*, as well as the part of the archetypal stud, didn't hurt the actor's blossoming image.

The Roman Spring of Mrs. Stone was just the first of a series of disappointing decisions made by Beatty. He chose his movies carefully, not needing to agree to projects he didn't like for the money alone, since his asking price had risen to $150,000 a picture after *Splendor in the Grass* and he thought nothing of rejecting a $200,000 offer that didn't meet his requirements. He was not only fussy about his own role in any project he considered; he also picked and chose on the basis of who would direct and who would star opposite him.

His decision to star in *All Fall Down*, which he made in 1962, was undoubtedly influenced by the fact that his mentor William Inge had written the script, adapted from a novel by James Leo Herlihy. John Frankenheimer directed the film, which again cast Beatty as young stud who brought heartache to an older woman, sensitively played by Eva Marie Saint.

Though the picture was a flop by anybody's standards, Warren's performance was impressive and was praised by many critics. Again, his image was nourished by the part of the selfish, cruel young man who used women only to cast them away when they were no longer needed.

It was during the filming of *All Fall Down* that Beatty's reputation started going from bad to worse, with the crew reportedly detesting him so much they locked him in a Key West jail where they'd been filming a scene and threw away the key.

Now the columnists had a field day reciting lists of the brazen young star's outrageous demands.

For starters, he demanded a star's dressing room at MGM, then refused to list his real name. The building directory read:

LAURENCE HARVEY

RICHARD WIDMARK

MARLON BRANDO

HENRY FONDA

GLENN FORD

GREGOR KROCP

PAUL NEWMAN

Beatty didn't help matters by explaining, "It was an invention of a friend of mine. I said I didn't want anyone to know which was my dressing room. I wanted to sleep."

The implication that he was more likely to be annoyed by fans than such established stars as Fonda, Newman, and Brando struck some Beatty-watchers as winsome, but the majority considered this the height of conceit. To add insult to injury, the dressing room that he had demanded—and received—was the best on the entire lot, the one usually reserved for Gregory Peck, who had never felt the necessity of hiding his identity when in residence.

One tantrum followed another. It's the custom for special visitors to be allowed on the set during filming. But Beatty would have none of this, and one day he simply retired into his dressing room and refused to come out until the set was cleared of visitors, holding up production and getting chastised for his unprofessional behavior.

Instead of downplaying his actions, the headstrong young man spoke testily in his own defense. "If you work better in absolute silence, you damned well should have absolute silence," he snapped. "When there's whispering and shuffling on the set, I get edgy. It affects my concentrating. The better known an actor becomes, the more obstacles are put in his path just trying to do an honest day's work."

Nor did he see any reason to ingratiate himself with the crew, no matter how much they disliked him for his indifference. "All right, so I'm not buddy-buddy with the crews," he agreed defensively when queried by a *Saturday Evening Post* reporter. "I don't get paid to be friends with them and they don't get paid to be friends with me. Making pals of grips and electricians is not an actor's most important job on the set. I think there's a tendency among some stars to make a popularity contest out of it." It didn't appear to have crossed his mind that perhaps actors make a point of being pleasant to the technicians simply because it makes their own lives easier.

Reporters, sick and tired of trying to pry good copy out of a newcomer who would greet the press with "I'll answer twenty-five percent of your questions," got their revenge by chronicling every obnoxious utterance that escaped his full, petulant lips. And on this score, he rarely let them down.

When he was being considered to portray the young John Kennedy in *PT 109* (a role taken up by Cliff Robertson after Beatty turned it down), Jack Warner suggested he go to Washington, D.C., to study the president and become acquainted with his mannerisms. "If the president wants me to play him," Beatty retorted, "tell him to come here and soak up some of *my* atmosphere." Since J.F.K. was regarded as the next thing to a saint at the time, Warren's remark amounted to near sacrilege.

The people who suffered most from Beatty's demands and opinions were the directors with whom he worked. According to his friend Robert Towne, "If the director was indecisive, Warren would absolutely destroy him. He'd ask so many questions—and he can ask more questions than any three-year-old—that the director didn't know whether he was coming or going. I think Warren's drive to be a producer was that he feared he would get into more films where the person in authority didn't quite know what he was doing."

In *Lilith*, released in 1964, Beatty found himself matched with a director who could be all too easily destroyed. Unknown to the actor, director Robert Rossen was already in the grip of a terminal illness. *Lilith* would be his last picture, and his last experience with the young leading man was so horrific that he allegedly told several close friends that when he died, it would be because working with Beatty had killed him.

This time, Warren couldn't get away with his boorish attitude on the excuse of being young, since his co-stars, Jean Seberg and Peter Fonda, were little more than kids themselves. And they were united in their mutual dislike of their co-star.

In the film, Beatty played a man who gets a job as a nurse in a mental hospital, where he falls for a nymphomaniac patient (played by Seberg) and ends up seeking admission to the hospital as an inmate himself. Word filtered out from the set early that working on *Lilith* wasn't unlike being in an asylum itself. And the name usually mentioned when blame was cast for the discordance was, of course, Warren Beatty.

Once again, Beatty went out of his way to alienate the cast, the crew, the director, and the press. When journalists visited the set, Warren turned his back on them so he could walk over to Rossen to discuss an involved scene with the director; then he quickly obliterated the portrait of a serious young actor by asking, "Do you think my hair is too long behind the ears?"

With three previous motion pictures to his credit, Beatty could no longer be considered wet behind those ears, and he made enemies right and left. Seberg, who gave a magnificent performance (especially under the tense circumstances) was convinced Warren was doing everything to undermine her work and grab the attention himself.

Beatty also had to contend with the antipathy of Peter Fonda, and the two almost came to blows more than once. In fact, so great was Fonda's loathing of the other male star that Beatty reportedly had to be spirited away from the New England location as soon as the filming there was finished, missing the wrap party for the cast after word got out that Fonda planned serious physical damage to Beatty's person. As it was, Fonda and friends had to be content with ripping apart Warren's unoccupied trailer.

And yet, in spite of the tensions and hostilities so prevalent on the set, Beatty's performance in the film stands out, showing his ability to portray a complex neurotic character.

In 1965, Beatty was on the screen in yet another flop, but in this instance, time has proved his choice to be the right one. *Mickey One* is now considered a classic of the American *film noir*. Like *Lilith*, it is only now receiving appreciation as a masterful film ahead of its time; of the two, it is considered by far the better work.

Interestingly enough, even the critics who liked the film knew it would not be a hit. Gene Youngblood, writing in the *Los Angeles Herald-Examiner* on January 9, 1966, called *Mickey One* "most likely the best American film of the year," then went on to explain, "This is not mass audience 'entertainment.' It will probably lose money at the box office and anger most viewers. But then so did 8½ and *L'Avventura*."

Mickey One, directed by Arthur Penn, a man who would become Beatty's close friend, is a grim fable about paranoia and survival. Mickey, a small-time Chicago cabaret entertainer, is certain that he has offended the Mob and goes underground to hide. At the film's end, the viewer still doesn't know whether the nightclub comic was mad or correct. Nor is the division of reality and fantasy especially important in terms of the film's motif.

What *is* important is the film's message: the need to go on in the face of all odds. Whether the paranoia is imagined or springs from a genuine cause, the fight to win is paramount. All this is symbolized by the Chinese junkman who appears again and again, beckoning to Mickey. When finally unmasked, he is no evil figure but the creator of a self-destructive Junk Art work entitled "Yes," a complicated Rube Goldberg-like construction that clangs and bangs and finally explodes as its meaning—"Courage is freedom"—is explained. The film ends as its protagonist finally realizes the aptness of this slogan in terms of his own life. He freely chooses to cease running away, and his life is no longer in danger. Whether or not it ever was in danger is irrelevant.

There's no question that the film was far ahead of its time. Its stark, stylized nightmare quality gives it a distinctly un-American feeling; its technique lies closer to Europe, to the films of France and Italy. Also, the paranoia that was later to engulf the country (and which has still not dissipated) was little more than an undercurrent in 1964. Kennedy had been assassinated by Lee Harvey Oswald and the Warren Commission's report was already in dispute, but most Americans still preferred to take whatever came at face value. A decade later, Beatty would star in *The Parallax View*, a simpler and less satisfying film but one that was more readily accepted by the public, who were now ripe to have their paranoia fed and vindicated.

The reception of *Mickey One* was a great disappointment to Warren, who had believed in this film to a much greater degree than any other movie he had made thus far. After five years and four films, he was dissatisfied and disillusioned. His ambition had not brought him the laurels he'd hoped for, and though he was adored by strangers as a sex symbol, he was rootless, with no ties or personal commitments.

Since coming to Hollywood, Warren had lived in a succession of hotels and dated a never-ending stream of pretty starlets. But none of this had brought him happiness. In fact, he once confessed, "Sometimes I wake up about 4 A.M. and I'm scared for a minute because I wonder where the hell I am."

Friends saw him as wondering where the hell he was in more ways than just geographically. As William Inge remarked, "He's been so intent on this career that he's devoted his entire self to it. He's just sitting around now, waiting for the rest of his life to come back to him."

He did not find the impressive roles he felt were his due as an actor in the next couple of years. But he did find love again. And he found the chance to do what he now wished to do more obsessively than ever: to be a producer.

6

A BADLY
ORGANIZED GUY

Beatty was accused of a multitude of negative traits during those early years in Hollywood, but never did anyone characterize him as indecisive. Like all young actors, he surrounded himself with paid retainers, but he rarely asked for anyone else's advice where artistic decisions were concerned. Instead, he relied upon others to deal with the mundane details of stardom.

His day-to-day finances were handled by employees. So unconcerned was he with his own financial accounts that, when he opened a suitcase in the middle of an interview in 1962, a total of thirty-five checks he had never bothered cashing fell out. He treated his accounts payable with the same indifference as his accounts receivable. When reminded of the unpaid bills littering the floor of a car he was driving, he shrugged, insisting, "I can't be bothered with things like this. I keep telling these people to send their bills to my business manager if they want to get paid."

The plodding, calculating side of the actor emerged only when confronted with artistic decisions. Deluged with scripts as a hot young box office attraction, Beatty still found the time to read each offering three times before coming to a decision. "If I find I don't want to read it the third time, then we've had it with that one," he explained. The number of scripts he hasn't wanted to read for the third time in his twenty-odd-year career in motion pictures is legion.

Not that the actor as a young man was all solemnity or sulkiness. At times he acted as any other man in his twenties might have had he become rich and famous overnight.

He loved Los Angeles, though he refused to commit himself to settling there long enough to sign a lease on a house or apartment. "Nothing's old out here," he crowed enthusiastically when he first arrived. "You want old, go back to New York."

He was already becoming famed for his propensity to jump on an airplane and jet anywhere on the spur of the moment; he worshiped the telephone, thinking nothing of making one transatlantic call after another just to chat. "He can make sixty-five calls in three hours and plan anything," director Mike Nichols, a longtime friend, has said, and more than one eager interviewer became quickly discouraged when the star spent most of their allotted time together taking and making calls.

His enthusiasm for burning the candle at both ends was boundless, but he never allowed it to interfere with his work (except quite early in his career, when he'd bore the press by bragging about the late hours he kept). "I'm a kind of badly organized guy," he mused in his younger days, not sounding ashamed of it at all. "I live a kind of kaleidoscopic existence, which can change from season to season. In New York or London, I may stay up all night every night. Then I come out here [to Los Angeles] and get a lot of sun and exercise. If I tell you now what I like to do, I may feel different at ten-thirty tonight!"

He basked in his own unpredictability, and, with youthful zest, gloated over all the options opened to him by success. "I waste a lot of time," he said happily in 1963. "I like to be able to waste that time by myself. Time is like ice cream. I love ice cream. I eat it all the time.

"I don't like to tie myself down to things. I have a certain resistance to sustained commitment. Maybe it's the disease of the day. What are we going to commit ourselves to?

"I'm really indulging myself, in a way. I really enjoy not to have to go out. I will probably have dinner by myself tonight."

Not that filmdom's newest superstud spent many evenings alone. Between his serious relationships, Warren artfully played the role of footloose bachelor to the hilt, exuding (when he wanted to) the kind of sexual charm that later caused the normally objective film critic Molly Haskell to remark, "You want to kiss him with your eyes open."

Many beautiful women wanted to do just that, and Beatty wasn't averse to making himself available. When he stayed at his friend producer Charles Feldman's Manhattan townhouse, he would invariably tie up the telephone for hours on end, calling one girl after another. And each lady would get the same greeting when she answered the phone. "What's new, pussycat?" Warren would ask, giving Feldman the title for a movie that would make millions with Peter O'Toole playing the suavely irresistible playboy.

And yet, fickle though he might have been, part of Warren seemed to feel the lack of a serious relationship. When Earl Wilson questioned him on the subject of marriage in the early 1960s, and asked if Beatty thought he'd ever take the plunge, the actor was unusually reflective. "Will I ever be married?" he repeated the question, holding his head as if in pain before finally answering, "I would say yes."

But when pressed by the columnist to come right out and say yes then, he was good-naturedly evasive, laughing as he refused to commit himself to that definite an answer.

Responsibility was the bugaboo he wished to avoid, and with commitment of any kind came responsibility. "There's something enjoyable about living in one furnished room with no money and a sense of freedom" is how he summed up his preferred existence, an existence he feared success may have destroyed forever. "Now there's responsibility and a lot of demands on your time and your freedom is very restricted. You lose your wonderful anonymity," he fretted.

And yet he showed no signs of turning his back on his fame, admitting in practically the next breath, "But there's a part of me that likes that kind of thing very much. Any actor who says he doesn't like it is a liar."

Leslie Caron was a most unlikely woman to share the life of

someone so footloose and frenetic. But then, Warren has never fallen in love with the likeliest choices.

The daughter of a French pharmacist and an American former ballerina, Leslie Caron was born July 1, 1931 in Paris. In appearance, she was more fragile than even the delicate Natalie Wood, carrying (at her heaviest) a mere 112 pounds on her fine-boned 5-foot 3½-inch frame. But the wispy brunette who had captured the hearts of Americans as the gamine in *Gigi* had a strong will as magnetic as her enormous eyes, generous mouth, and elfin heart-shaped face.

She hadn't been raised to be a clinging vine. "When I was five," she has recalled, "my mother put a brush into my hand and said, 'From now on, you comb your own hair.' Since then, I've always made my own decisions. I've never had somebody who was willing to make my decisions for me." By the time she was in her teens, she was already a dancer with the Ballets des Champs Elysées. Soon afterward, she was a married woman as well.

Her first marriage, to an American, George Hormel, heir to the meat-packing fortune, was short-lived, and, publicly at least, she shed no tears at its demise. "When love is over," she said succinctly of her divorce, "it should be broken off at once."

Still, she didn't shy away from making commitments, and not long after her divorce was final, in 1956, she married again. Her new husband was a celebrity in his own right. Englishman Peter Hall was the director of London's Royal Shakespeare Company, and during their marriage Leslie lived with him and their two children in London.

So quiet were Warren and Leslie when they met and began seeing each other that no one even detected a breath of scandal when Hall and Caron separated. After all, show business matches break up right and left, and there seemed nothing newsworthy to this estrangement.

And then Hall dropped his bombshell. Hearing that Leslie planned to take their son and daughter to the West Coast, he panicked, afraid she intended to keep them there and away from him (a charge she denies to this day). He filed for divorce, accusing his wife of numerous instances of adultery in Chicago, Jamaica (where she filmed *Father Goose* with Cary Grant), and Beverly Hills. He named Warren Beatty as corespondent and asked that the court enjoin Leslie from taking Christopher John, seven, and Jennifer, five, out of Great Britain.

Leslie herself was not in England when Hall filed the divorce action. She and Warren were registered, in separate suites, at the Beverly Hills Hotel when news of Hall's charges reached her. Stunned by her mate's turning their private lives into public gossip fodder, she could only murmur that she was "too shocked to comment" when asked for her reaction to the suit. Beatty, meanwhile, kept a low profile and a closed mouth.

Just about everyone else was talking, though. Adultery didn't provoke much interest in Hollywood, where it was as common as Mercedes-Benzes, but getting caught at it was something else. That was news, and it was reported in this instance with a salaciousness that often went beyond the bounds of mere gossip.

Leslie and Warren refused to stoop to the level of the popular press, nor did they act sheepish or guilt-ridden. "Warren and I are in the open," Leslie commented in the midst of the divorce action. "We are not hiding from anyone or anything. We are very much in love, and people have to get used to it. . . ."

But love wasn't everything, and Hall's battle for custody was an ugly hindrance in the romance. "I would be completely happy," Leslie admitted, "except for this coming battle with the children. I want to take my children back with me to Hollywood. I have a very good school for them there."

Warren was struggling with another problem as well. He was finally coming to terms with the image of himself he had helped to create. When interviewed last year by Aaron Latham for *Rolling Stone*, Caron reminisced about her relationship with Beatty. While she was filming in Jamaica—and still married—Beatty hid out, rarely leaving her house lest it be discovered that he was on the island with her (and little dreaming their stay on Jamaica would be one of the instances of adultery later cited by Hall). Sequestered together day after day, Leslie and Warren spent a great deal of time in serious talk. His conversation, she recalled, centered mostly around Marlon Brando, Montgomery Clift, and himself. He saw the three of them as a trinity, equally gifted as actors, and yet he was well aware that the public and critics did not put him in the same league with the other two men.

"He was considered just a playboy," Caron told Latham. "He had spent too much time wooing women in the public eye. Of course it bothered him that he wasn't taken seriously. We used to talk about it. He was in despair about it."

Certainly, he didn't help matters with his next two movies: *Promise Her Anything*, opposite Caron, and *Kaleidoscope*, with Susannah York, both in 1966. Later, Beatty vaguely referred to this period by saying, "There was a certain amount of turmoil in my private life then. I had to make some pictures, and I made them. I had to make them in England, and so I did."

The "had to" obviously refers to his love for Caron. When Leslie was required to be in England, Warren was by her side, sharing her five-story Georgian townhouse overlooking the formal greenery of Montpelier Square in Kensington. It was during this year that he made *Promise Her Anything* and *Kaleidoscope*, both rather dreary comedies, because, as he later confessed, he "had to" be in London.

There is no doubt that Warren returned Leslie's love for him. In the summer of 1965, columnist Sheilah Graham asked him the question that was on everyone's lips at the time. "Are you going to marry Leslie?"

For once, Warren gave a forthright answer. "Whenever she wants to," he said with disarming frankness. "I will marry Leslie when she says 'Now!'"

Unhappily for the lovers, Hall won an injunction in June of 1964 to keep both the children in London temporarily, while Leslie attempted to explain that she'd never intended to keep the children out of England permanently. The injunction created a mutually unsatisfactory situation for both parents, with the children put in boarding schools.

Leslie became a constant transatlantic traveler, jetting back and forth between Los Angeles and London to visit Christopher and Jennifer. The scandal and the threatened loss of her offspring were horrible to live with, but when a headstrong Frenchwoman falls in love, there's no turning back. "I am greedy," she revealed candidly. "I want to live while I'm alive." Still, the prospect of living without her children was frightening and depressing.

Through all the turmoil, Warren, that once egocentric, immature gadabout, was nothing but supportive and loving. He said nothing publicly, but he paid all court costs in the legal battle with Hall.

Finally, months after the divorce went through, custody of the children was awarded to Leslie. Joyously, she and Warren made plans for the future.

Beatty was determined that the Hall children should be content and comfortable in California and the tension of the custody tug-of-war should be forgotten by them as soon as possible. To this end, he rented a beautiful house for $3,500 a month, with three swimming pools and two tennis courts for the children.

The seeds—planted early in his career—that led Warren to become a producer were now germinating. It had been disillusioning enough to be an actor when he believed in the films he was making and had a personal commitment to his work. Now, starring in vehicles he knew to be pedestrian from the start, he was sure he must look beyond performing for satisfaction. "When I would fly in from Europe," he later confessed, "it was embarrassing for me to put 'actor' on my landing card."

Of course, his drive toward producing was motivated by more than a disinclination to admit he was an actor. Acting in itself was no longer enough for him, if it had ever been. And he saw no reason to look outside of the movie business for gratification. Earlier, when discussing the chance that he could have succeeded as a professional pianist, he had said, "But I believe everyone has a limited amount of creative libido or whatever you want to call it. If you put it into too many things, it dissipates itself."

Turning to production was natural for a perfectionist—some would even say a nitpicker—like Beatty. He yearned for control, and even as an actor, he tried to take over as much of it as possible. During the filming of *Lilith*, for example, he demanded that his character's line "I've read *Crime and Punishment* and *The Brothers Karamazov*" be changed to "I've read *Crime and Punishment* and *half* of *The Brothers Karamazov.*" In his eyes, it was a justifiable request, since he felt that the character, as written, would not have been able to read both books in their entirety.

It was his consciousness of story lines and character development that served as the greatest impetus toward turning producer. The man who had been such an avid reader as a child explains, "Once I became interested in stories and getting stories told, I realized I had to be a producer to get them told in the right way."

But for the time being, his involvement with Leslie overshadowed his own ambitions. He was happy with this woman who respected his desire for total honesty, who could be totally vulnerable yet embraced a concept of personal freedom and self-satisfaction as all-encompassing as Warren's own. He adapted himself to the requirements of her life, her love for her children, her need for socializing, even hosting weekly parties to indulge her love of entertaining.

His adoration was returned in full. "He is a great actor—and I love him madly," she told a friend when discussing Warren. Then, after a pause, she happily corrected herself without abashment. "No, put that the other way around. I love him madly—and he is a great actor."

With Warren to bolster her, she flourished, looking lovelier than ever in spite of the unpleasantness that had touched her life. The story is told of Leslie attending a party in California without Warren. Natalie Wood was at the same gathering, and when someone remarked to her, "Leslie is looking so beautiful," Natalie offered an immediate one-word explanation.

"Warren," his ex-love pronounced succinctly.

However, the relationship that brought such glowing happiness to the principals did not end in marriage, and no one has ever been quite sure who actually broke it off, though the generally accepted version had Leslie deciding against a third marriage and Warren carrying a torch for years to follow. In retrospect, his affair with Caron fulfilled Warren's requirements for satisfaction, as it was certainly "a very short relationship where you tell the truth to somebody"—something he has stated ". . . is in many ways more satisfying than a longer relationship where the truth becomes painful."

As for Leslie, she did not remain unattached for long. She remarried in 1969. Husband Michael Laughlin (they are no longer together) was the producer of the film *Joanna*.

And if Warren lived up to his own stated requirements for a relationship, Leslie was one of those of whom actress Lee Grant, of *Shampoo*, may have been speaking when she said, "Warren's conquests of women are not totally successful. His percentage is about fifty-fifty. Those he can't conquer don't want to be part of a crowd— one of Warren's girls. But the Peter Pan quality in Warren is very attractive to some. He teaches them to fly, and they have extraordinary experiences with him. Then they grow up and go on, and he keeps flying. Like Peter Pan, he always comes back to another little girl who's ready to fly off with him to Never-Never Land."

In this case, Warren flew off not just to one other "little girl," but to a whole string of them. He wasn't prepared to get seriously involved again in a hurry. His romance with Caron had been detrimental to his career, and right now it was his career that concerned him most. Love would have to take a back seat until he had made the transition from being just an actor to succeeding as an actor and a producer.

7

A "SOMETIMES" ACTOR

As an actor, Warren has gained as much renown for the roles he didn't accept as for the ones he did. And on the subject of just why he turned down many of the plum parts he was offered during the sixties and early seventies, he maintains a reticence that makes him appear downright loquacious where his love life is concerned, refusing to discuss many of the movies he has rejected with an unrewarding, if dignified, "I don't think it's very nice."

His "no" has meant a big break for another actor on more than one occasion. In fact, one Hollywood joke has it that Robert Redford owes his stardom to Beatty, because he rose to fame in roles the other actor had rejected. Some of the films Warren was wanted for but didn't want (in some cases, just because he didn't want to read that script a third time) are *The Adventurers*, *The Ski Bum*, *Ryan's Daughter*, *The Godfather*, *PT 109*, *Murphy's War*, *Butch Cassidy and the Sundance Kid*, *The Great Gatsby*, *Last Tango in Paris*, and *The Sting*.

Today, a millionaire many times over, Beatty can shrug off his legendary unavailability. Those periods of turning down film after film, he says, were "positive times, not negative. I was simply too busy to work in them."

For the most part, as an actor, Beatty has concentrated on making "quality" motion pictures. As a youngster starting out, he made one movie after another, all of which left him feeling let down in some way. It's understandable that he should say, "Movies are only a part of my life. I don't see any particular need to make movies all the time if I don't feel like it. I really don't look upon myself as an actor. An actor acts. I do think of myself as a sometimes actor. I don't like to evaluate my experiences merely in relation to the profession of movie acting. . . . If you take movies too seriously, if you think it's important to turn out a bunch of hits . . . well, that's kind of a boring way to live."

Not only, he believes, is it boring; it's futile as well. Acting, in itself, doesn't give Warren pleasure but acting in a worthwhile film does. "What I enjoy about working in movies," he explains, "is expressing something I want to say—doing those movies I *want* to make. Maybe it's unfortunate that I became a movie star. It's afforded me such a luxurious life that I've never completely turned away from it and gone on to make only the films I really want to make. There's always been the feeling 'Well, I'll keep a finger in it as a movie actor. It's all sort of a silly machine, but I might as well jump in once in a while, so that I'll still be invited.'"

He does explain why he hasn't done certain movies. For instance, he told Dick Adler he turned down *Butch Cassidy and the Sundance Kid* because he "didn't feel much like getting on a horse and riding around. . . ." Besides, he preferred making *The Only Game in Town* for George Stevens, one of his favorite directors. He thought *The Sting* wasn't very interesting and didn't get past page fifty of the script (by this time, he was offered too many scripts to give each one the requisite three readings). On viewing the finished film, he announced that he still didn't think it was very interesting, except for the good ending. *The Way We Were* (another break for Redford) would have had him playing a character he deemed "apathetic." He originally turned down *The Great Gatsby* because he wished to renegotiate the contract; by the time he'd decided to do the film, Redford had already been signed.

He's said of *The Godfather* that he didn't think he was right for the part, played on screen by Al Pacino, because he wasn't "Italian enough," which shows he learned some kind of lesson from *The Roman Spring of Mrs. Stone*. Also, at the time he was offered many of these roles, he was deeply involved in George McGovern's cam-

paign for President, a commitment that affected his acting career
even more intensely than did his relationship with Caron.

As Beatty approached thirty, it was clear that he was a different
person from the surly actor he'd been in his twenties. He was just as
determined to succeed on his own terms, but the terms themselves
had undergone a metamorphosis. He was looking for a story to
make his own, to produce. And he was no longer interested in
making any pictures, as a producer or an actor, that did not command his full interest. This side of Warren has survived unchanged
through the years. As he himself explained in the mid-seventies, "I
was offered *The Godfather* to produce and act in. It looked to me
like a sure hit, but I couldn't get interested. I'm interested in original
movie scripts . . . not usually in making books, plays, or musicals
into movies, or in remakes of movies."

During the period of his life preceding *Bonnie and Clyde,*
Beatty was, more than ever, an enigma to his fans. Superficially, he
was living the playboy role to the hilt, but beneath that frivolous
exterior, he was solemnly plotting his future in the film business.

These two sides to Warren's character have always existed.
With the years, he has perfected his ability to integrate the public
image with the private man. As director George Stevens explains it,
"Warren is quite a deception. He really *is* the iceberg, because what
you see of him on the surface is no part of him at all. He seems
lighthearted, even frivolous. But he's scholarly, headstrong, stub-
born, and tough, and he knows as much as I do about filmmaking."

In 1966, the less scholarly side of the man was most visible.
Beautiful girls passed in and out of the Beverly Wilshire Hotel in
Beverly Hills at all hours of the day and night, coming and going
from the El Escondido penthouse suite Warren inhabited. "Suite"
makes Warren's longtime lodgings sound more extensive than they
were. A visitor took the hotel elevator to the ninth floor, then walked
up a flight of stairs to a black-lacquered door. Behind this door lay
two tiny rooms, usually in a frenzy of disorganized clutter. Newspapers, scripts, books, and stacks of opened and unopened mail lit-
tered every available surface and overflowed onto the floor. The

private terrace was bigger than the entire apartment, and it was here that Warren might watch television, eat a tray lunch, or contemplate a script while his latest beautiful guest sunbathed.

He shunned ties with a vengeance, sticking to his permanent hotel suite when he was in California and putting up at the St. Regis, the Carlyle, or the Delmonico when he was in New York. His cars were rented; his meals eaten in restaurants or sent up by room service; his wardrobe expensive but minimal. Everyday details were attended to by employees, in keeping with his belief that "Obstacles can eat you up. I think sidestepping them is better than trying to deal with them." With his women and his stacks of scripts, he had enough on his hands.

His wariness of the press had increased, undoubtedly in part because of the tawdriness with which so many journalists had treated his romance with Caron. He rarely submitted to interviews, which had so infrequently presented him in a positive light in the past. "Interviewers expect you to push in a plug, light up like a Christmas tree, and start throwing off witticisms and things," he had already complained in a rare talk with a reporter.

In his personal life, he was doing what he did so well—avoiding boredom. In his professional life, he was concerned with establishing himself as a producer and an intellectual, determined to shake off the inconsequential playboy image he'd wept over on Leslie's shoulder, even while refusing to discard the jet-set way of life that was part and parcel of his character by now and that continued to reinforce a reputation for superficiality and vacuity.

He had already discovered the vehicle that would bring him added fame, the respect he longed for, and enough money to relieve him of the burden of ever again having to do anything he wasn't one hundred percent committed to.

When he and Leslie Caron had still been well-nigh inseparable, they had flown back to Hollywood from Europe and attended a party together, a party at which a palm reader circulated. When she read Warren's palm, she told him he would be a murderer, a prediction that frightened Miss Caron.

Shortly after this incident occurred, he and Leslie went to Paris. As is the case when Warren falls in love, he was searching for a script suitable for Leslie and him to co-star in. Along the way, the two had lunch with French director François Truffaut.

Truffaut, an intellectual if ever there was one, and a highly respected filmmaker (*The 400 Blows*, *Jules and Jim*, *Shoot the Piano Player* [this film, starring Charles Aznavour, bears a strong resemblance to *Mickey One*] and *The Bride Wore Black*), was sympathetic to the lovers' quest.

He suggested Warren take a look at a script he himself was too busy to consider, a script that had been submitted by two young Americans and was called *Bonnie and Clyde*.

Today, Caron says it was she who persuaded Beatty to buy the script, as a vehicle to star the two of them (she says he originally wasn't interested because he thought the movie was a western). Certainly, it requires a flight of fancy to imagine the pert Parisian portraying gun-slinging Bonnie Parker. Be that as it may, Warren was finally convinced that *Bonnie and Clyde* was for him, with or without Caron. He bought rights to the script, deciding not only to act in the movie but to produce it as well.

Now that he'd found the property he wanted, Beatty was in no great rush to get it on the screen. This was his chance to show everyone that the celluloid sex symbol wasn't just two-dimensional, that he knew the film business as intimately as he'd known any of the women with whom the press had linked him. Though impetuous in affairs of the heart, Beatty never rushed as an actor or a businessman. He realized that if *Bonnie and Clyde* bombed, he might never get a second chance to convince studio heads and the world at large of his business acumen. So he went slowly.

As soon as it became common knowledge that Warren Beatty planned to produce a movie, there were many who waited eagerly for him to fail—as Warren was well aware. He'd offended some important people in his youth, not only the press (who presented him their "Sour Apple" award for the most uncooperative interview) but creative people and money men as well. It wasn't odd that some of them chortled at the prospect of the kid who was too big for his britches making a fool of himself. *If* he could even raise the money, that is. And some investors doubted he could even achieve that primary goal.

Furthermore, actors—especially gorgeous actors—were still expected to know their place. Though it's considered fine and dandy for actors to direct television shows (Jerry Paris, Alan Alda and Jackie Cooper are among those who have followed that course), the big screen, in a behind-the-scenes capacity, is supposed to be for pros only. When Robert Redford decided to direct *Ordinary People*, both the industry grapevine and the columnists kept track of every rumor that might spell disaster for the endeavor. Only when the film turned out to be a commercial as well as a critical success was Redford accorded any credit as a director.

Producing doesn't have as much in common with acting as directing does. Though the production end of the business isn't necessarily uncreative, art isn't nearly as important as bookkeeping and organization. The producer's function is managerial. He must raise the money to produce the picture, secure the talent, oversee script changes and editing, and worry over distribution. His realm is one of economics and ledger entries, and there are some producers who leave most of the artistic decision making up to their directors, limiting their own function to that of fund raiser, cost cutter and bill payer.

Warren didn't go into producing only to play with other people's money. He approached his budding career as a producer with a desire for total control over the property, a need to see the project through from start to finish. This approach has never changed, though it has intensified somewhat with each motion picture Beatty has produced.

And so he girded himself for the challenge of bringing what some scoffers were already writing off as "another gangster movie" to the screen. He knew he would have a myriad of decisions, and he knew there was only so much responsibility he would allow himself to delegate. Before he had any idea exactly what he was going to do with the Robert Benton and David Newman script, he knew it was going to be *his* movie. And he suspected, rightly, that the experience was going to change his life.

8

THE BARROW GANG
HITS THE BIG TIME

With *Bonnie and Clyde*, in 1967, Warren was well on his way toward realizing his longtime dream of controlling and manipulating the medium in which he chose to express himself. With a screenplay he purchased "for about $10,000," he set about making one of the most successful motion pictures of our time.

Robert Benton and David Newman were two young magazine writers from *Esquire* who had collaborated on their first screenplay, then tried to persuade François Truffaut to direct it. After the French director assured him that *Bonnie and Clyde* was not the western he'd assumed it to be, Warren returned to America. In New York, just a few days after his meeting with Truffaut, Warren telephoned Robert Benton.

Beatty told the young writer he'd like to read the script—as soon as possible. Straight to the point whenever his professional interest is piqued, Beatty presented himself at the door of the writer's Manhattan apartment a brief half hour later.

Interestingly enough, Benton did not give the fledgling producer the hard sell on his own screenplay. Instead, he warned Beatty that he doubted he would be interested in doing *Bonnie and Clyde*. As he and Newman had written it, the script detailed homosexual relations between Clyde Barrow and C.W., the friend and cohort of Barrow and Bonnie Parker. Benton was certain an actor with a rampantly heterosexual image like Warren's wouldn't be remotely interested in anything to do with homosexuality. Still, Warren insisted he wished to read the script.

He left with a copy of it, telephoning Benton later that evening to tell him he wanted to do the movie. When Benton learned that Warren had read only the beginning of the screenplay thus far, he assured him that after he'd read further, he would change his mind.

But as others had learned before him, Benton was to find out that when Beatty's mind was made up, there was no changing it. Beatty called back a bit later to tell the stunned writer that he had finished reading the screenplay and that he definitely wanted to do it.

The first obstacle surmounted, Beatty was now faced with more decisions, the first of which was whether he should direct the film himself. Faced with the double burden of producing his first motion picture and starring in it as well, Beatty wisely considered that signing himself on as director to boot might be biting off far more than he could chew.

But it was important for him to settle on a director he knew he could work with satisfactorily, someone who understood his outlook and aims and someone who could make the grim tale of the Barrow gang come alive, someone who could transform a bunch of punks into the stuff of poetry. It's not surprising he decided to contact Arthur Penn, the man who in *Mickey One* had so perfectly captured the atmosphere of a man on the run, who had turned hoodlumism into high art.

"It was a basic script that had been turned down by everyone," Warren later described his venture. "I could have directed it if I wanted to, but I decided it was better to go with another director and knew that I could collaborate with Arthur Penn."

His decision to go with Penn was one he would never have cause to regret, especially since it was Penn who persuaded Benton and Newman to rewrite the script, removing the homosexual elements to make the film more palatable to the general public. Penn and Beatty turned out to be an unbeatable combination, and Penn had nothing but praise for Beatty after the picture was completed. "He is really a perfect producer," he said with satisfaction. "He makes everyone demand the best of themselves. Warren stays with a picture through editing, mixing, and scoring. He plain works harder than anyone else I have ever seen."

Next, Beatty had to find someone to play Bonnie Parker. He had already met with Leslie Caron in Los Angeles to tell her she was not right for the part, a rejection that continues to rile the French-woman, who says, "The way he discarded me after I got him to buy *Bonnie and Clyde* was rather ruthless. . . . Anyone who has come close to Warren has shed quite a few feathers. He tends to maul you."

If Beatty hadn't "mauled" her in this instance, the critics un-doubtedly would have. There's no question that Caron was indeed wrong for the role. The question was, who would be right? He considered several actresses for the part of Clyde Barrow's female partner, including his former love Natalie Wood (who wasn't inter-ested, perhaps remembering what had happened the last time she'd starred opposite the actor), Carol Lynley, Tuesday Weld, and his sister Shirley MacLaine. He was almost ready to go with Sue (*Lolita*) Lyon when, again thanks to Penn's suggestion, he instead cast an unknown young actress in the role.

Faye Dunaway, an army brat from Florida, was tall, blond, and beautiful, with a tautness in her slender body that was in keep-ing with Bonnie Parker's daring and rebelliousness. A fashion model turned actress, Dunaway's biggest role to date had been the lead in *Hogan's Goat*, an off-Broadway show.

With a perspicacity that testified to his talents as a producer, Warren signed a host of other little-known players for the film's other major roles, all of whom excelled in their craft and went on to greater reknown. Gene Hackman, a hitherto obscure actor who later achieved star status with *The French Connection*, was cast as Clyde's brother, Buck; Michael J. Pollard played the clumsily clownish C.W.; and the gifted character actress Estelle Parsons por-trayed Buck's querulous wife, Blanche. In his brief appearance on screen as the hayseed suitor who revels in being kidnapped by the Barrow gang, Gene Wilder came close to stealing the show, going on to greater fame in *The Producers, Blazing Saddles, Young Frank-*

enstein, and other box office bonanzas, in addition to directing films himself.

Beatty embraced the chore of producing the picture with an energy that made co-workers feel anemic. As David Thomson later wrote in *Playgirl,*

> Like one of the great producers of the 1930s—Irving Thalberg or David Selznick—Beatty leaves nothing to chance. In some cases, he has an idea in mind for ten years before he thinks of a script. Those hours alone are spent in reading and research. Then he finds a writer and gives him as long as he needs to furnish the best possible script. Casting of parts and assignment of technical chores all interest him as much as his own role and the hunt for ideal locations. After the film is made, he goes into retreat to cut and mix it, emerging only to supervise every stage of the promotion. Nothing else in life seems to have fulfilled his obsessive energies as much as producing a film. He stakes his life and his fortune on it, and so far he has come away richer every time—which only means he can take a larger gamble next time.

Beatty as a producer has been compared to George C. Scott in the *Patton* war room. He demands the best from the people who work with him, expecting the standards of others on his films to be as high as his own. Whereas many producers will do what they can to speed up the production process, Beatty actively encouraged director Penn to shoot a scene as many times as he had to until he was sure it was right.

Beatty thrived on producing. It was new and exciting, and, most important, it was intensely challenging. With *Bonnie and Clyde,* he was faced, from start to finish, with the type of struggle that kept his adrenalin pumping and held boredom at bay.

Today, he admits that some aspects of production are little more than drudgery. But in 1967, he avidly attacked every nuance of the production end of the business. "I enjoyed it the first time, on *Bonnie and Clyde,*" he's said of producing, "because I wanted to see if I could play with the big boys. But, you know, they don't look that big after you've been playing with them."

They might have been giants to the neophyte producer, but like Jack the Giant-Killer, he refused to be intimidated by them—or to be deterred from his ultimate goal. Still needing a studio if *Bonnie and Clyde* was going to be made, he got down on his knees to beg Jack Warner to give him a chance. Though both Columbia and United Artists had already turned down the project, Warner, who told Beatty his pleading embarrassed him, finally agreed to give Beatty a deal.

That deal was one of the best Beatty ever made, since it allowed him to retain ownership of forty percent of the movie. Considering that in its first year of release, the film grossed $30 million, Warren had cut himself a sizable chunk of a very big pie.

When *Bonnie and Clyde* was originally released, it looked as though that pie might turn out to be humble. Warner Brothers had booked the movie in second-class theaters and was treating it as just another B feature. Business was slow, and the initial reviews disappointing. But Warren wasn't going to give up easily, and as soon as the first good reviews came in, he pressured Warner into pulling it from the theaters and reopening it in the best movie houses in the country, making *Bonnie and Clyde* one of the few films to have opened twice.

Nor did he sit back and trust the studio to give the film the promotion he felt it deserved. "I got out and sold the picture," he says of his personal efforts to promote his baby. "It's demeaning to an actor and it's taken a big chunk out of my life, and I didn't know a thing, but I learned."

He learned something he hadn't learned in all those years as an actor: how to woo the press, treat them with kid gloves, and have them eating out of your hand.

So he singlehandedly mounted his own campaign to resell his movie and get it rereviewed and noticed. He wasn't about to let it slide into obscurity without a battle. "He was a tiger," Arthur Penn remembers. "He was not going to let that movie not have its day."

As Warren saw it, he had no choice but to go down fighting if necessary. "From the first day of shooting," he explained, "I felt there was one thing I could never run away from in this film. No matter what was wrong with it, I was gonna step up and take complete blame for it. For a change, there wouldn't be any cop-outs."

The rest is now in the annals of cinema history. *Bonnie and Clyde* reopened as a smash. He had won respect as a producer, and that meant more to him than any praise for his acting abilities ever had. "I've been what they call 'bankable' as an actor ever since *Splendor in the Grass* in 1960," he told Dick Adler. "Very luckily for me, it was a hit, and I could pick and choose what I wanted to do from then on. But there's a difference between being bankable as an actor and being someone about whom people in charge of a studio will say 'Go ahead and let him make the movie however he wants to make it.' It's a matter of confidence in your ability to get it together in a careful manner.

"What *Bonnie and Clyde* really did was give me the opportunity to relax toward movies—in a financial sense as well as in the sense of knowing that if I ever wanted to make a particular movie from then on, I could just go and do it. Because of it, I've been able to refuse a lot of movies which I'd probably otherwise have wound up doing."

The film's phenomenal success was due in part to the sixties' disillusioned youth, who saw it taking up where Peter Fonda's *Easy Rider* left off, glorifying the antihero who lived outside society but, of course, had a heart of gold. It is debatable whether the real Clyde Barrow possessed this feature, or much of a heart at all, for that matter. But movies embrace art and not reality, so Bonnie Parker and Clyde Barrow had to be polished up and turned into cult heroes if the film was going to draw an audience.

On its first release, the movie's publicity played up the angle that this was the story of bank robbers who got away with the money, but in Beatty's opinion, there were deeper reasons for the film's ultimate acceptance by the public. The time was right for *Bonnie and Clyde*, just as the time would be right for the canny producer's *Shampoo, Heaven Can Wait*, and *Reds*.

"I guess it was appealing then to see a film about a time when the banks were foreclosing on people," Beatty said a decade later. "It was an unfair society then [in the Dust Bowl thirties] and the unfairness of our society was something that people were becoming aware of in the middle sixties. There was a lot of racial unrest, and the war in Vietnam had eased up to a point where the unfairness of it all was pretty obvious.

"So there was a certain sympathy to the characters of Bonnie and Clyde for being the sort of Robin Hood-ish way they fancied themselves. Whether they were that way in fact is another question."

The deck was undeniably stacked on behalf of the desperados. The film's Bonnie and Clyde are not only a great deal more physically attractive than their real-life counterparts, they are also presented as good-hearted youngsters infatuated with glamor and excitement, who decide to rob banks much as a youngster today might decide to become a rock singer, as an escape from an existence which promises to be bleak unless drastic action is taken.

The movie's lawmen are grim and humorless in contrast to the compassionate, light-hearted Barrow gang, who are portrayed as the film's true victims. The murder and mayhem that followed in their wake was accidental if not somebody else's fault. As with Eva Peron in *Evita*, their crimes are consistently whitewashed to make them more palatable—and resoundingly commercial.

Still, Beatty didn't actually deserve the charge that he was glamorizing a life of crime. The glitter and the energy, the sheer zest of the finished film, with its upbeat bluegrass soundtrack, was what made it glamorous; Bonnie and Clyde themselves were shown as lonely, hunted vagabonds who lived in hiding until they were finally massacred in a police ambush.

Warren had no patience with those who assailed the movie for its violence, taking to task the venerable *New York Times* film critic Bosley Crowther, who attacked *Bonnie and Clyde* for its gratuitous butchery. With a hauteur worthy of his assertive past, Beatty denigrated the "old maid" critics who had found fault with his product.

It was too bad not everyone liked and appreciated the film, Warren agreed coldly, "but Bosley Crowther is not my mother."

More than fifteen years have passed since *Bonnie and Clyde's* release, and we have grown so accustomed to the most blatant, tasteless movie carnage that it's difficult to remember, or accept, the furor that greeted the movie's violence. But at the time, the graphic depiction of Blanche Barrow receiving a bullet in her eye, Buck getting the top of his head blown off, and Parker and Barrow writhing in slow-motion balletic grace as they are riddled with bullets was enough to shock all but the most jaded audiences.

Wisely, Beatty did not deny the violence in the film, but he insisted it was necessary and never gratuitous. "Some critics have called *Bonnie and Clyde* a glorification of violence," he said. "We wouldn't have gotten ten nominations if the people in our business felt that way. My director, Arthur Penn, and I felt each scene of violence made a moral point."

The ten Academy Award nominations made their own point: People could no longer dismiss Warren Beatty as just another pretty face. Beatty himself was nominated for Best Actor; Faye Dunaway, as Best Actress; Gene Hackman, Best Supporting Actor; Michael J. Pollard, Best Supporting Actor; Estelle Parsons, Best Supporting Actress; with other nominations for Best Picture, Best Direction, Best Costume Design, Best Cinematography, Best Story and Screenplay Written Directly for the Screen.

Neither Beatty himself nor the picture won an Oscar (though Estelle Parsons did), but *Bonnie and Clyde* had accomplished what its producer desired. He had come up a winner his first time out. He had shown the "big boys" he could play their game. His triumph with *Bonnie and Clyde* won him a reputation as an astute filmmaker; equally important, it legitimated Beatty in his own eyes. No longer a callow, untested youth, he now possessed the maturity and tolerance so sorely lacking in his past.

9

THE "NEW" WARREN BEATTY

The Hollywood brat was gone forever. In his place was a man, only thirty, who had mellowed and matured and who, in spite of his unchanged reticence toward the press, was suddenly their darling.

One of the few actors to receive both the Sour Apple Award and the Golden Apple Award form the Hollywood Women's Press Club, Beatty's new popularity with the press establishment was the result of a change in his personality. He wasn't opening himself up a great deal more to journalists than he had in the past, but now he maintained his privacy with good grace and a lack of hostility.

No longer an insecure, unseasoned actor, Beatty now glowed with self-respect. *Bonnie and Clyde* had brought about a change in his outlook.

Those days of being ashamed of his profession had ended at last, and he could finally say ". . . I'm proud of being an actor. Didn't used to be. It took me a long time. What gives me pride about the profession of acting is that I now know so much more about other professions."

As a producer, he had also learned a great deal more about filmmaking. The man who had once refused to be friendly with film crews now saw that filmmaking must be a team effort in order to be successful. "There are two components," he said, speaking of what makes a good filmmaker. "The person who initiates things well and observes things well. A good director or filmmaker must have both ingredients. I try to create a situation where everyone's anxious to take part. There's no denying that films are made by a group." He at last understood that the better the relations within that group, the better the finished product. He had come a long way from the arrogant tyro who couldn't have cared less about alienating his fellow workers.

For the first time since he'd arrived on the West Coast for his screen test, Beatty was humble. He was not afraid to admit ignorance, not even to reporters, who, of course, loved him for his modesty. "I've often felt I knew a lot about this business," he told *The New York Times.* "But I really don't know anything about it at all. Matter of fact, I don't know if I'll even stay in acting. One thing I can tell you, though. I've revised my opinions about nearly everything I thought two years ago."

One of the traits of his new style was a delightfully self-deprecating sense of humor. He could laugh at himself now, and he actually encouraged others to laugh with him.

The new, lovable Warren Beatty stole the show when he spoke at a 1968 testimonial dinner for songwriter Sammy Cahn. Warren was on the dais with a host of other celebrities, all of whom had made typical speeches praising Cahn's kindness, generosity, and talents.

When it was Warren's turn to speak, he told the assembled VIPs, "I've known Sammy Cahn for a long time now. I have a speech I prepared and I'd like to read it now. 'I want to thank my director, my mother, my father, and my sister, and the friends of my mother, my father, my sister.'" The audience dissolved into laughter as they realized Warren was giving the acceptance speech he would have made if *Bonnie and Clyde* had won the Oscar for Best Picture or he had been named Best Actor.

His success enabled him to joke about things he had taken with deadly seriousness in the past. He could relax, no longer having anything to prove. Now he could poke fun at himself instead of touting his own virtues. "Actor Warren Beatty," he remarked wryly after the release of *Bonnie and Clyde*, "thought his producer was just wonderful."

Beatty even viewed his Don Juan reputation with, if not a sense of humor, a sense of resignation. "You know," he sighed, "people have been trying to marry me off to every girl I've been out with in the past fifteen years. But I'm not signing any contract. It's become kind of a game now. I can handle it. I love to hear people trying to make me say things. Yes, I actually enjoy it."

He had never identified with the man he'd been painted to be, but he was no longer desperate to convince the world that he wasn't that media-created being. He accepted the reality of being a star.

"There are those who think they know Warren," his *Bonnie and Clyde* co-star Faye Dunaway (never romantically involved with Beatty) said, "but very few people do and few ever will. He has been hurt by those who persist in viewing him as some moronic super-stud. Yes, women and sex are very important to Warren, but so are many other things. This man is multidimensional, but he reserves himself for a chosen few."

The new Warren could in no way be described as an inter-viewer's dream. For one thing, he has always been slow and decisive in his speech, punctuating sentences with random "er"s, "um"s, and other sound effects. His opinions were given slowly, with a great deal of deliberation, leaving talk show hosts with the hope that he would finish at least a sentence or two between commercials.

He also had a tendency to break off in the middle of a sen-tence, leave thoughts unfinished, and pepper his conversation with totally irrelevant comments that often took the interviewer's mind off the subject at hand. He loved dropping odd bits of information into serious conversations. "Did you know that in London," he sud-denly announced in the midst of one interview, "every twenty min-utes a man is hit by a car?"

In writing up the results of her interview with Beatty for the *New York Post* in 1963, Judy Michaelson perfectly reproduced the actor's speech pattern. In speaking of his sudden success following *Splendor in the Grass*, Warren said, "A guy goes along, he's living over there on twenty-four dollars a month"—here he paused to make a sweeping gesture in the general vicinity of the West Side of Manhattan—"and the thing has a certain . . . He's trying to do a good job . . . boom, boom, boom, it all comes out and you lose your enthusiasm. . . . I became repelled by the idea of working. I quit work. . . . What is this, the sociological study of a young actor? *Boring.*" Such a plethora of broken sentences and incomplete thoughts made it difficult for even the most inventive journalist to come up with a decent story.

The producer was as closemouthed on the subject of his notorious romances as the actor had always been, explaining, "The reason I don't discuss the girls I've known or my private life is because there are always other people involved. I'm a very normal guy. But I've made one rule for myself. Never tell lies to women. And I've always told my girlfriends the truth, however painful it might be to both of us. That's the only way to get an honest relationship."

The "new" Warren Beatty didn't seem especially interested in a long-term relationship of any sort, though. His taste in women has always been eclectic, and though the more famous ladies have invariably garnered the publicity, there have also been hundreds of unknowns who have been wooed by Warren—waitresses, secretaries, writers, photographers, Hollywood hangers-on. The pursuit clearly holds more attraction than the capture.

In 1967, writing in *Esquire* magazine, Rex Reed (who was decidedly not charmed by Mr. Beatty) quoted an anonymous friend of the actor's as saying, "Warren wants the entire world to want to go to bed with him. And what he really is unable to take more than anything else in life is rejection."

The anecdotes centering on Warren as a Lothario are endless, and certainly many of them are apocryphal as well. But somewhere beyond the myth lies the truth: that Warren adores the chase and that variety is the spice of his life. He has sent roses to girls he's known for five minutes, has invited perfect strangers to visit his rooms, and has, though some women would find it difficult to believe, been turned down.

When asked once if the idea of being irresistible to women appealed to him, Beatty lightly answered, "If I thought it were true, it would appeal to me very much. It's a wonderful idea—would that it were true."

And Warren's disclaimer to being welcomed with open arms by every woman he meets is backed up by at least one objective source. Former Los Angeles bureau chief for *The New York Times* Steve Roberts recalls one time when Beatty didn't score. "In those days," says Roberts, "I had a very attractive assistant. Beatty pursued her relentlessly. He called her so often, he was driving her crazy. I told her, 'Think how many women would love to be in your position.' She said, 'Think how many have been.'"

Throughout the 1960s, Beatty's reputation as a hypersexual womanizer continued to blossom, though he himself tried to shrug off the idea that he might be a victim of his own image.

"I'm not like James Bond, with an image to keep up," he insisted. "I've been the same all my life, and I don't see why I should change now."

In truth, he did have an image from his earlier films, and even his portrayal of the less than manly Clyde Barrow (Beatty was, in actuality, fascinated by Barrow's impotence and inability to consummate his passion for Bonnie Parker) couldn't take the gilding off the lily, not when his offscreen actions attested that his own faculties were unimpaired.

Whenever possible, he attributes his well-documented promiscuity to a deep affection for the opposite sex, though he has always been very much "one of the boys" as well, palling around with playboy cronies like Jack Nicholson and Hugh Hefner. While insisting he has never distinguished between men and women as friends, he admits he has a tendency to trust women more, though he's also admitted, "I'm not sure that I'm a hugely trusting person."

With his new acclaim as a producer, more women than ever made themselves available. Now, besides being handsome and famous, Beatty was also powerful. And power, as Henry Kissinger told us, is the ultimate aphrodisiac.

Warren had matured enough to wear his new status comfortably, even casually, but some aspects of it continued to astound him. "I think that's idiotic . . . the power," he admitted. "You have it in your job, you know, and that makes people play up to you, and it's very seductive. You get in deeper and deeper. It's very much the same as being a big star. They all want you. They say, 'Shall I send you a print of my movie or my wife?'"

Beatty was not to be so easily bought. Having proved his point with *Bonnie and Clyde*, he was now prepared to bide his time before rushing into anything, especially another production commitment.

And, with his newfound wealth, he could well afford to be even more selective as an actor. "I haven't done too many films, because I only make the pictures I want to make," he has said. "I don't feel any responsibility to give the public what it wants, either. Why should I? You can't work like that. If you try and guess what the public wants, you go crazy. You've just got to go ahead and do what interests *you*."

It would be eight years before Beatty ventured out again as a producer with *Shampoo*, and in that time, he completed only four films as an actor.

He starred opposite Elizabeth Taylor in *The Only Game in Town*, mainly because his friend George Stevens was directing, with the $1,200,000 salary he received for his work giving added impetus (after all, there's no such thing as *too* rich). Neither a commercial nor a critical success, this lackluster tale of love among the losers is nowadays easy to catch on late-night television.

Two years later, in 1971, Warren starred in "$" for director-writer Richard Brooks, who would later direct Beatty's attention to Diane Keaton in *Looking for Mr. Goodbar*. "$," in which he starred opposite Goldie Hawn, was an extremely entertaining caper film, made on location in Germany. It was lighthearted fun with an ingenious plot. As Archer Winston, reviewing the movie for the *New York Post*, pointed out, "What makes the caper so inspiring is the fact that its hero, Joe Collins (Warren Beatty), is a protection specialist in a Hamburg bank which is the repository of illegal funds of gangsters, gambling czars, drug dealers and such. He feels no moral compunctions in working out a method of stealing from people who can't ask the police to get the money back."

Though it was not especially popular in America, the film was a hit in Europe. Today, it is still a cult classic in England, and it is certainly funnier and friskier than most efforts of this genre.

The third movie starring Beatty during this period was *The Parallax View*, an offshoot of the *Mickey One* school of paranoia, though this Alan Pakula vehicle pointed a finger directly at the bad guys (the government). Like *Three Days of the Condor*, another venture in the "whose side are they on?" field, *Parallax View* took a promising premise and turned it into turgid, confusing fare. It was, however, the closest thing to a politically slanted movie made by Beatty before *Shampoo*.

The other film Warren played the lead in during this pre-*Shampoo* era was the best of the bunch. *McCabe and Mrs. Miller*, Robert Altman's gritty film of 1971, teamed a bearded Beatty as the gambler McCabe opposite Julie Christie as the world-weary madam "Mrs. Miller" in an existential story of the Old West.

McCabe and Mrs. Miller is a bleakly romantic classic, its cinematography a montage of muted grays and blues, its love story cynical, its Leonard Cohen soundtrack ironical and haunting. In it, Beatty turned in one of his finest performances. As the bluff entrepreneur whose dreams of riches end in violence, he was both touching and heroic, and no one who has seen the film will ever forget the last bleak images, as McCabe's body is engulfed by the snow while the woman he loved loses herself in bittersweet opium dreams.

McCabe and Mrs. Miller is notable not only as one of Beatty's finest moments as an actor and one of the last films he was to make for any producer but himself. It was also his first screen performance opposite Britain's Julie Christie, the woman who appeared destined to become Mrs. Warren Beatty.

10

"WHAT A STRANGE GIRL!"

Julie Christie was born April 14, 1941 in Assam, India, where her British father was a tea planter. Nine years later, at the age of eight, she and her brother Clive were sent to England for schooling, and she attended a series of British boarding schools.

She had to attend a series of schools because, even as a child, she was clever and unpredictable and was expelled from one of those schools, the educational arm of a straitlaced convent. "Yes, that's true," she readily agreed when asked about her expulsion years later. "It was so silly. I was expelled for telling dirty jokes to an absolutely horrible little girl. She told on me and her parents threatened to take her away because they said I was poisoning her mind!"

At sixteen, as is the custom with British schoolchildren, Julie took the seven O-level exams necessary for graduation from secondary school or promotion to the next grade (students who continue their education go on to take A-level examinations). When she failed French, her parents sent her to France to live with friends of her mother's as the logical approach to gaining proficiency in the language.

In speaking to journalist Helen Lawrenson about that cultural adventure, Julie was enthusiastic, remarking that ". . . it was a marvelous experience. I changed completely. Life really began for me in France. I don't think I existed, actually, until then. I was just a schoolgirl, pretty obnoxious—oh, I was awful, really! I'd never met any intellectuals or people who were unconventional. All I knew was English boarding-school life, and then I suddenly found myself

living with a wonderful huge family—very intellectual and sophisticated about life. The father was writing a dictionary of the Basque
language—and they were all so damned eccentric it was wonderful.
They used to fly into great family rages and shout at each other and
of course I had been used to all that stuffy English restraint. At first I
was unhappy and it was hell. I was so homesick. But then their life
began to rub off on me—and there were lots of dances and parties
and all those French boys, much more attractive and more intelligent than the English boys."

She returned to England, where she passed her A-levels, then
drifted for a bit, attending Brighton Technical College. She says she
started studying drama at the Central School of Speech Training
and Dramatic Art in London because "I didn't really know what I
wanted." Acting appealed to her, however, and she spent three years
at the school before getting firsthand experience with the Frinton
Repertory Company in Essex. After drama school, she also did
some modeling, though at five foot four and 112 pounds, she knew
she had no future in the fashion business.

Her first break was getting the lead in an English sci-fi drama,
A *for Andromeda*. This was followed by small parts in two films,
Crooks, Anonymous and *The Fast Lady*. And then—nothing.

"I was nearly going out of my mind," she told Lawrenson,
"and the worst of it was that I was mixing with a lot of successful
people—Terry [Terence] Stamp and people like that of my own age
who were all making it big. I began to feel terribly inferior. I'd think,
'Oh, I'm so thin and my feet are so big and I'm such a dull girl.' I'd
go to a party, and I'd be so frightened. People who met me used to
say, 'What a strange girl.'"

Those were lean days, and Julie's life in London was much like
any other struggling young actress's. At one point, money was so
tight that she couldn't even afford a place of her own. Instead, she
lived on an air mattress, begging for places to sleep. "I would turn
up at even the remotest friend's place and ask for floor space," she
recalled ruefully after success had assured she would never have to

do so again. "A cupboard. *Anything.* God, it was awful moving around with my little mat."

Her real break came when John Schlesinger cast her in a small role in *Billy Liar*, his gentle, delightful tale of a Walter Mitty-ish young man who inhabits a fantasy world. Though Julie was on-screen only a short time in her film debut, her role was a pivotal one and her performance memorable. When the movie was released in the States in 1963, Julie was singled out as one of the freshest new talents to cross the Atlantic.

Schlesinger, who was won over by the brash, kooky twenty-two-year-old (he had originally felt she would be all wrong for *Billy Liar* and had been averse to casting her in the part), now became her staunchest supporter, and it was he who cemented her stardom by giving her the lead in his study of life amidst the jaded jet set in *Darling* in 1964.

The role of Diana Price, the flighty young model whose life is examined in *Darling*, was a demanding one for a relatively inexperienced actress. It was a demanding experience for the gray-eyed, blonde Christie. Not only was she required to be onscreen for almost the whole two hours of screen time, playing opposite seasoned professionals like Laurence Harvey, she was also aware that Schlesinger had had to fight to get her the lead. The money men backing the film had wanted a different actress for the role. Interestingly enough, their choice had been Shirley MacLaine.

Darling was a smash, and Julie's public espousal of many of its protagonist's iconoclastic values was a built-in publicity booster. "I can enjoy almost any sensation," she caroled ardently. "When a toothache or a chilblain is gone, I miss it. I live as though I'm going to die tomorrow. All the time, I see how short life is. It is today—now—that counts for me."

"Now" at the time included a young man of eclectic talents with whom Julie lived openly. He was a twenty-four-year-old lithographer and part-time art teacher who had met the then unknown Miss Christie when, working as a part-time mailman, he had delivered a letter to her.

Julie referred to her romance as "a special relationship," making it clear whenever she was asked that the two had no plans to marry. Marriage, she said, in a statement that might have sprung from the lips of Warren Beatty, she considered to be "a peculiar talent," one which she likened to writing or composing music. "I certainly don't think I have that talent," she confessed guiltlessly.

Julie and her lover shared a flat in the West Kensington section of London with another friend, a girl named Nicky Croke, who was employed in the advertising department of a publishing company. Their apartment was a typical young peoples' pad of the mid sixties, decorated with a combination of modern furniture, castoffs, and bargains from the Portobello Road antique stalls. A giant Union Jack hung in the front hall.

If her values were much like Diana Price's, Julie's life wasn't; it was inconceivable to her that she might choose the chic, frantic, and fashionable scene that was *Darling's* milieu.

"For one thing," she explained, "none of my friends would have the energy for all that kind of flash, switched-on existence. We're the laziest lot of people, content to sit around and watch television and play records and talk and decorate our homes. I'm very proletarian in my tastes. I love modern jazz—pop music—and I love dancing, so I go to clubs like the Ad Lib and the Flamingo, but most of the time I just muck around with my friends."

While "mucking around" in the early 1960's, Julie happened to be introduced to Warren Beatty. Beatty was then sharing Leslie Caron's Knightsbridge townhouse, Julie was in love with another man and there was no sign that she and Beatty would ever be more than casual acquaintances, especially since Warren was, to all intents and purposes, an advocate of the kind of "flash, switched-on existence" that left the pragmatic earthy Englishwoman cold.

Even after winning the Academy Award for Best Actress in *Darling*, Julie remained true to her man. Still, she shied away from legalizing their commitment. "I don't imagine I'll ever want anyone but [him]," she said in 1966 (just a year before they broke up and she hooked up with Warren). "But marriage—it's like signing your life away."

A one-sided success can strain any relationship, especially when that success carries the fame and notoriety that goes hand-in-hand with winning an Oscar. But Julie, right up to the end, didn't think the change in her status would affect her relationship.

"Oh, but his values are my values," she was quick to insist. "Besides, he isn't just an art teacher. He's a painter, a good painter. The most important thing in any man-woman relationship is for the man to be the dominant one. This is what [he] and I have, and I can't imagine our ever letting it change. Marriage sort of frightens me, though. We've talked of it, of course, and we've talked about having children. . . . I don't know. . . . I don't go around with movie people. My friends are writers or artists—a lot of them are graphic designers—and I simply can't imagine myself becoming a 'movie star' type. If I can do the films I want to do—and I intend to do *only* the ones I think are right for me—and also keep on in the theater (I'd love to play Hilda in *The Master Builder,* for example,) and not lose my perspective at all those dreadful, corrupting, astronomical sums of money film people flash at you, then I think I can work out my private life. Anyway, I'm going to try."

She tried, but life wasn't the same after she had been touched by stardom. *Darling* had turned her from a raffish hippie into everybody's darling, and not the least of her admirers was Warren Beatty. "I've always loved her on the screen, beginning with *Darling,*" says the man who remained one of her biggest fans and closest friends even after their love affair was over. "You don't have enough room in your article for me to tell you why. I like her even when she's in a bad movie. *Demon Seed* was bad, and I still loved her."

The rest of the world learned that Warren loved her in 1967. Julie was in San Francisco shooting *Petulia,* starring opposite Richard Chamberlain, and it soon became obvious to even the dimmest observer that Beatty was spending an unwarrantable amount of time commuting between that city and Los Angeles.

Leslie Caron—who had just received an Oscar nomination for *The L-Shaped Room* when she was first introduced to Warren—at a party thrown by Freddie Fields at Beverly Hills' The Bistro—offered an interesting, if unproven, insight into her ex-lover's taste in women when she told Aaron Latham, "Warren has an interesting psychology. He has always fallen in love with girls who have just won or been nominated for an Academy Award." As he would later become Diane Keaton's suitor after she picked up her coveted statuette for *Annie Hall*, so he now became the only man in Julie's life. The art teacher was completely out of the picture.

"I don't think men see any lusty sexiness in me," is how Miss Christie once described herself. "The appealing thing is an air of abandonment. Men don't want any responsibility, and neither do I."

In Beatty, Julie seemed to have found the perfect mate. It wasn't long before the two people who refused to make commitments were inseparable. When Julie had finished *Petulia* and gone on to Geneva to shoot *In Search of Gregory*, Warren wasn't far behind. He was omnipresent, even hanging around the set for hours on end when she was working. His behavior was the same when Julie was filming *The Go-Between* in the English countryside with Alan Bates and Edward Fox. Sure enough, Warren flew to London to be nearby.

The two were undeniably well matched, with a great deal in common as well as being unalike enough to remain alluring to each other.

Both shunned responsibility and were equally uninterested in marriage. Both were private people, almost secretive about their lives offscreen. Both were intelligent and perceptive. And both refused to get trapped by material possessions or the seductiveness of the limelight.

"I'm not a myth or a legend," Julie explained, "just somebody who works in films. I don't do anything public. I try to live a private life when I'm not working. I couldn't care less about publicity, and I suppose a star is someone who cares about that very much. I find it torturous and agonizing to have to talk about myself to strangers."

Of course, though Warren has always insisted he doesn't care about being a star with a capital "S," the fact of the matter is that he is and has always been exactly that. He's got that larger than life glamour that is what being a movie star is all about. And he's a much more complex person than Julie.

Robert Altman got to know them both very well when he directed them together in *McCabe and Mrs. Miller.* Beatty and Christie shared a small cottage on Vancouver's Howe Sound and isolated themselves from most of the cast and crew, but they spent a lot of time with Altman, whom they both liked very much. Altman saw the two of them as being very different indeed. "For one thing," he said, "Julie doesn't *like* being a movie star. All she wants is to act. If she had her way, she'd like to have a nice role in a play or in a film that does not require a lot of recognition. This is very genuine with her. Warren, on the other hand, is so many things in addition to the superstar that he is and feels [he is]. He is also the businessman, extremely astute. The director. The writer. He is very strong and cares about what he does."

Though Warren has never flaunted his wealth and continually insists he would live much as he already does if he should lose all his money, he pursues a far from rustic existence. He has always stayed at the most prestigious hotels, leaned toward expensive clothes (he may wear a pair of jeans but chances are the jacket accompanying them will have a pricey Italian designer's label in its lining), and frequented exclusive restaurants. His rootlessness is displayed in hopping on a jet plane, not roughing it in a trailer. On the other hand, Christie actually does live minimally; *Shampoo*'s costume designer Anthea Sylbert once described her as someone who would "live in a log cabin, drive a truck and wear overalls if she could." This is no exaggeration, either. Since she and Warren split up, Julie, when not working, has spent most of her time on the farm she owns in Wales, leading a most unglamorous life.

The similarities between Julie and Warren meshed with their differences, and the result was an ideal if impermanent union. His relationship with Julie further mellowed Warren. He was more human than ever before.

The outspoken, unaffected English actress had captivated one of filmdom's most eligible bachelors and, no matter how either of them said they felt about marriage, the world at large was sure they would wed.

Though Beatty insisted, as ever, that he was not the marrying kind, he made no attempt to hide his feelings for his new flame, not even under the most harrowing circumstances. While filming "$" in Hamburg, Beatty came close to losing his life but not to losing the thought that was uppermost in his mind.

During a scene shot in a railroad freight yard, Beatty slipped, lost his balance, and fell on the tracks. Director Richard Brooks and the rest of the crew watched in helpless horror as a freight train approached the track upon which Warren had fallen, too far away for them to reach him in time. Dazed, he could only stare at the oncoming train at first. Then, just in the nick of time, he came to his senses and pulled himself out of danger.

At St. George's Hospital, he was treated for painful injuries, including a torn ligament in one ankle. As a German admitting clerk filled out the forms for admission, Warren sat grimacing in discomfort, answering the questions dutifully and with no interest in the proceedings—until asked if he was married. Than a grin wiped the pain off his face as he replied, "No. But I'm in love!"

In love he was, and openly proud of his loved one. For the man who once described an ideal relationship as one where "a man tells the truth to a woman, a woman tells the truth to a man," Julie was made to order.

"She's almost pathologically honest!" he said happily. "It's there when you just look at her. She's beautiful by all your conventional standards. And I admire her work. So it's no surprise that I love her. She's also an important actress."

She was, in short, perfection. And, even though their love is over, Beatty still sings Julie's praises whenever he's given the chance. Of all the women in his life, he admires her the most. In 1975, after the two had co-starred in Beatty's *Heaven Can Wait*, he said of Julie, "Her own preferences don't lean to the linear film, and she's decidedly not sentimental. She'll always tell you what she thinks, with clarity and the directness of an arrow. The pain, too. But it's valuable. And whatever it is you sense about her is what holds the film together—that intensity you feel about her."

The intensity of his feeling for her in the earlier part of that decade was evident—though Warren, the man who likes to boast that he's skilled at dodging questions, never spoke at length about his beloved. "What we have is privacy," he said when pressed for a comment, "and if that disappears, what's left?"

Not that "no comment" was all it took to still tongues. The rumor ran rampant that the two had married in secret during the filming of *McCabe and Mrs. Miller*, a rumor that neither would dignify with an outright denial. Warren, as was the norm, said nothing, though Sheilah Graham revealed that he "playfully" speared her with his knife and fork when, during a breakfast together, she ventured to ask him if Julie was around.

Julie herself just shrugged off the rumor that she and Beatty were man and wife. "If we are, we are" was her only comment. "If we're not, we're not."

The press even went so far as to track down Julie's mother, Rosemary Christie, at her home in Wales to question her on the possibility of a secret wedding. "If I knew, I would not say," she commented disappointingly. "It's private."

And then, in 1973, just when everyone was waiting for the two to announce their marriage, Julie went off—without Warren—to Venice to star in Nicolas Roeg's *Don't Look Now* opposite Donald Sutherland. Suddenly it was clear that the romance was over.

There were no fireworks, no public announcements. But soon Warren was publicly squiring other young ladies about town, and the truth was plain to see. Neither would discuss the demise of their liaison, though several of Warren's friends ventured the opinion that

Julie would have been happy with a conventional relationship and couldn't put up with Warren's compulsive womanizing, which had continued even when they were living together.

"If Julie and I ever split up, I'll pay her alimony," Warren once promised, "if she wants or needs it." But the relationship that was the closest thing to a legalized marriage he's ever had ended with Julie asking for nothing and with the general consensus being that she would have actually married Warren (who had reportedly asked her several times to be his wife) if he could have made the commitment to settling down.

Regardless of the differences that led to their split, Julie and Warren remained close friends, and she has since starred in two of producer Beatty's films—*Shampoo* and *Heaven Can Wait*—opposite actor Beatty.

Reporter Marvene Jones, who early in her career had been subjected to Beatty's charm, was one of many who felt Julie had never lost her affection for the man, though she had lost her ability to put up with his relentless skirt-chasing, an activity one of his ex-girlfriends likened to "a sport with him."

Marvene Jones remembers an encounter with Christie a good while after she and Warren had split. "I did an interview with Julie Christie for my show at RKO," Jones recalls. "I happened to catch her at a cocktail party, and she didn't know a camera was going to be there or anything. *Shampoo* had just come out. I said, 'Julie, did you do *Shampoo* because of Warren, because of your friendship with Warren?' And she said yes, that she did it because Warren had asked her to do it, and she said that Warren is 'a very good promoter.' I felt that she still loved him very much and had a hang-up about him. . . ."

Since *Shampoo*, Julie has made few films, choosing instead to spend most of her time at her farm in Wales, eschewing the glittering sphere Warren has never ceased to inhabit. She still refuses to comment on her longtime relationship with Beatty.

Beatty didn't mope around after he and Julie went their separate ways. He went back to doing what he's always done best, dating a string of beautiful women. But this time he had an ace up his sleeve. While the world was gossiping about Warren Beatty as a modern-day Don Juan, he was preparing to produce a motion picture about just that subject. With *Shampoo*, Beatty would have the last laugh, and a very profitable one at that, on the topic of the compulsive womanizer.

11

DON JUAN
AT THE BOX OFFICE

In 1967, flushed with triumph over his first venture as a producer, Beatty had already begun looking for another property to produce. Though he went on to act in other people's films before taking the plunge again, he had already, the year *Bonnie and Clyde* came out, acquired the script for what would be the second motion picture produced under his auspices.

Its title was *Keith's My Name, Hair's My Game,* and it had been written by Robert Towne, a young friend of Warren's. It would undergo a great many changes before finally being brought to the screen (there were no political overtones in the original script), with the final screenplay credited to Robert Towne and Warren Beatty, making *Shampoo* the first of his films in which Warren worked closely with his writers.

Beatty was drawn to the story because it showed that "even the promiscuous feel pain"; certainly, its political considerations were never foreseen to be anything more than a subplot, though the burnt-out desperation and clutching at straws in the political arena that saw Richard Nixon as the Great White Hope of America is an apt metaphor for the hidden hopes of the promiscuous: this, at last, might be the real thing.

Once he'd decided to jump in and tackle the project (never one to rush things, Warren kept the script shelved but not forgotten for several years), the producer gave it every moment of his waking life. By the time the final script was called for in 1973, Beatty's work-aholic tendencies were once again in full swing. He and Towne were closeted together for eleven days; when they emerged, it was with the shooting script for a movie titled *Shampoo.*

"I just wanted to get the subject out of my system." Beatty said of his desire to do a film concerned with a character composed of so many traits attributed to himself. "People can make what they want of it. There's a lot of me in every character I play. And I think that all of us have to close out that promiscuous phase in our lives. But, in a lot of ways, George is simply not me."

Clearly, Warren was thinking of himself—or at least himself and people he knew—when he spoke of "all of us" having to close out a "promiscuous phase" in life, since he's far too intelligent and well informed to view the heartlands of America as a hotbed of promiscuity. However, while his words didn't exactly constitute a sociological truth, they aroused interest. And interest, after all, is what makes people go to the movies.

And many people went to see *Shampoo* in the hope of learning what makes Warren Beatty tick. The film offered no explanation of George the hairdresser's womanizing (or Warren on any level). Nor was it an apologia for promiscuity, though it painted George in rather attractive colors. "I wanted to challenge the assumption that a hypersexual character with women, a Don Juan, is a misogynist or a latent homosexual," Warren defended his protagonist. "As for comparisons between George and me, I'm not offended." On the contrary, he seemed to invite comparisons.

Rather than viewing George's manipulations of the women in his life as cold and cruel, or his choice of vocation as one which allows a male professional domination and control over a woman (through her looks, a sensitive area with most women), Beatty saw George as a man motivated by his very affection for womankind.

"I wanted to make him a hairdresser from the beginning. He's around women, touching women, wanting to make them beautiful, not to degrade them. To many women their hairdresser is a source of the truth. He sees you when your hair is done and not done."

Beatty's view of his own movie seems rather naive. Certainly, the beauty business is one that preys on women's sense of insecurity

and reinforces the concept that how a woman looks is more important than what she does. And George the Sex Object is not viewed
as *just* that by any of the female characters in the film, all of whom
display a greater degree of emotional involvement with George than
he does with them. Nor, at the film's finish, do any of the women
end up seemingly happier than does George. One (Lee Grant) ends
up alone; one (Goldie Hawn) with a weak-willed boy producer; and
one (Julie Christie) with a fleshy, tiresome man much older than
she.

Warren seemed blind to the women's getting short shrift, concentrating instead on George's being used by them for sexual pleasure. "Men over thirty have a hard time accepting *Shampoo's* easy
acknowledgment of the fact that there are women today to whom
men are merely sex objects," he insisted, avoiding the other salient
points raised by the film. "They're upset, unsettled by the theme
that says promiscuity is no longer just for males, that there are
women who enjoy uninvolved, unemotional sex encounters."

On the other hand, according to him, women delighted in
what he saw as George's dehumanized status. When asked if the
role he played in the film was close to his own reputation as a
Lothario, he glibly replied, "I guess it is. But, you know, I find
feminists and women's libbers are more happy about it than anyone
else. Surprised? Not really. Feminists are delighted at having a stupid male sex object they can talk about."

What Warren failed to see was that George wasn't regarded as a
"stupid male sex object" by any of the women in the film. Not only
did they consider him worthy of their adoration, he was also smart
enough to string them along. And he never told where he had come
up with the misguided notion that feminists preferred males to be
sex objects when, in fact, the women's movement preached that no
human being should be regarded as such.

"I think sex is a serious subject," stated the man whose public
life and press clippings could be read as a direct contradiction to that
avowal. "And therefore the film is a serious subject."

And Beatty did take his film as seriously as any auteur, guiding director Hal Ashby with the same doggedness he had applied to Arthur Penn during the making of *Bonnie and Clyde*, expecting the cast and crew to share his commitment to the project, and losing patience with audiences and reviewers who failed to see the serious side of the subject he was presenting.

"It's not a frivolous movie," he insisted, infuriated with those who saw it as such. "It's a movie about frivolous people, and not only exists as a comedy of manners, but there's also a rather sad undercurrent."

The sad undercurrent was presumably Julie Christie's leaving George at the movie's end, unable to put up with his promiscuity, though she was the one woman he was capable of loving. This was another aspect of the film he refused to discuss in detail, telling one interviewer, "If I knew you, if I trusted you, I could sit down and answer that question in possibly an extended way and try to give you some idea of how much I relate to that character. But I don't." And that was that.

Despite the producer's moralizing on the subject of sleeping around, the fact remains that *Shampoo* is an entertaining satire, a genuine comedy of manners brought into focus by the 1968 election-night festivities around which the story revolves.

As co-writer Robert Towne explained, "It's about people who settle for things," pointing out that, in contrast to the political climate pervading the film, "nobody mentions voting or having voted. The television is on with actual TV footage from the election but nobody seems to notice." Beatty, who voluntarily retired from filmmaking to devote himself to politics in 1968, was using his first film since that retirement to express his disillusionment with the nation's political indifference.

Though he didn't come right out and say it in so many words, Beatty had been as disappointed and let down by the political sphere as he had been years before by movie stardom. Politics, he had learned firsthand, was a frustrating business.

"You have to pull in and out of politics," he said after he had pulled out, "otherwise you can exhaust yourself, particularly if you're not a professional. It's hard to see results in politics. Years ago, in the days when Bobby and King and everybody was shot, Senator [Joe] Tidings introduced a bill on gun control. The polls were eighty-five percent in favor, but it got totally watered down."

The watering down, the hypocrisy and lying that takes place in politics as well as in sexual relationships is what led Beatty to make *Shampoo*. When Tag Gallagher, discussing the film with its producer for *The Village Voice* in 1975, asked why Beatty set the film in 1968, he answered unhesitatingly, "Don't you think that was the turning point of the sixties? Turning point for George, too. I think that's when the American people came face to face with who they really were, with what they had permitted. I should say, what we had permitted, you, *The Village Voice*, I had permitted. It was the end of a lot of dreams of the early sixties, and the morning after that election, for me the prospects were pretty grim. I think the prospects for George are pretty grim in his life, the morning after this exhausting night, and George seems to be maybe ten years older than the night before, and tired, really rather degenerate. . . ."

What drew Warren to politics in the first place, to the interests that motivated him to campaign for George McGovern, to make *Shampoo*, to spend ten years obsessed with making *Reds*?

"I don't want to live my life in movies," he once said vehemently. "They're fun, but they're not a cure for cancer." Being a movie star has simply never meant much to Warren, and the more he uses his fame for causes he considers worthwhile, the less shame he feels at being an actor. He's motivated, even driven, by a deep-rooted need to be something more.

Dick Adler asked Beatty, around the time *Shampoo* was released, if he agreed with the statement of another actor who had said that making movies was basically a female occupation because "you lie on your back and let them do things to you." Beatty's answer is revealing.

"First of all," he said, "I don't think females are necessarily people who lie on their backs and let things be done to them; it says a lot about the sex life of a man who thinks they are. I think that a certain amount of enforced narcissism *would* appear to be a tool of the trade: wondering how you look all the time—not so much pretty, but correct for the part. I never think of acting as particularly feminine or passive, but then, I'm not really a good person to ask— I've only made fourteen movies in fourteen and a half years, and half of those were made in the first three years of my career. I've spent, I figured out the other day, something like seven years just turning down movies. Obviously, there's something uncomfortable for me about making them."

The political world, he found, was less narcissistic. It was, he said, "easier to do political interviews because they're really about something else. . . ."

He has always preferred discussing politics to discussing films for just that reason. When it comes to talking, he would rather talk about politics than anything else.

"That's because politics *is* talk," he explains. "Politics is conversation, compromise, clarification, and discussion. But when you talk about movies, there is something antithetical to the whole doing of it. Movies should talk for themselves. I hate to read myself quoted about a movie. I hate to say, 'This is what that meant.' It's like trying to describe what an expression on your own face means."

As an actor, he found it relatively easy to make the switch and become a political spokesman and organizer, and he didn't find his career stood in the way of being taken seriously.

"I haven't had any trouble being taken seriously, at least not for the last ten years," he said. "As to why actors tend to get involved in causes, you have to remember all the people who are constantly pestering an actor to do various things. He may reject nine out of ten of them, but the one he does accept invariably causes certain people to call him self-serving. This was something I felt very often during the McGovern campaign. I was continually stepping out of the way—worried about being attacked in print for exploiting my position. Actually, I was only accused of that once that I can remember, but it made me very angry at the time."

In the long run, Beatty's campaigning brought him greater respect and admiration than he'd received as an actor. One of those most vocal in their praise of Warren as a political supporter is George McGovern himself, who says, "He took a year out of his life to do it. He traveled around the country making speeches, debating issues, interpreting me to the public, and he personally was responsible for raising more than a million dollars. His ideas were shrewd and his advice valuable. He has a political maturity astounding in someone so inexperienced—the instincts of a man who spent a lifetime in politics. But I think what startled me most about Warren was learning that he is so deeply human."

Beatty's work for McGovern was not his first experience in campaigning nor was it his last. He had zealously supported Robert Kennedy and Hubert Humphrey earlier, and later was an active worker for Jimmy Carter's election, when he saw that the mood he had recreated in *Shampoo* was becoming entrenched. "What I feel," he said in 1978, "is that there is a general and dangerous mood in the country of people withdrawing from trying to help one another, that is manifested in the so-called tax revolt in California, the lack of interest in the Equal Rights Amendment, and a general reactionary turn throughout the country.

"I think people are getting into a dangerously selfish mood, and they will pay a price for that. We will pay a price for that. I think Carter has had the unfortunate position of having to deal with that and with a Congress that seems to be answering the tax revolt mood of its constituents by abandoning welfare projects and other areas in which the government is the only hope for the improvement of life of those less fortunate.

"People are giving up on solving society's problems, and for that reason, I think we need well-organized leadership for valid liberal causes. And I think Carter is developing this ability."

Those words, spoken six years ago, show Beatty to be a reliable political prophet, since 1983 shows the country taking, for better or for worse, an even more pronounced swing to the reactionary right. He cannot be greatly surprised that gun control, a cause for which he worked actively as a member of John Glenn's Emergency Gun

Controls Committee in 1968, has achieved no significant legislative gains.

As a political organizer and campaigner, Warren displayed the same orderliness and determination that has made him such a successful motion picture producer. He willingly threw himself into the center of the struggle. As Pierre Salinger, former press secretary for President Kennedy, who worked side by side with Beatty during Robert Kennedy's presidential campaign, recalls, "Some actors play at supporting candidates for the publicity they can get out of it. In the Robert Kennedy campaign of 1968, Warren was a 'guts' worker, not a movie star. He read every speech Bob had ever made in the Senate, and when he talked to hostile kids on college campuses, he won them over as skillfully as Bob himself did."

A skilled campaigner, a professional-level politico, an enthusiastic barnstormer—this side of Warren was new and unexpected to many of his fans. But once Beatty took the political floor, there was no doubting the seriousness of his political commitment. And the obvious sincerity of his alignment to the liberal cause, along with the unmistakable political overtones of *Shampoo*, was enough to nurture the suspicion that Beatty intended one day to follow the example of a leading man from the silver screen of the 1940s and toss his own hat into the ring.

12

OF POLITICS
AND SEXUALITY

"Politicians today are the real stars, aren't they?" Warren Beatty has been known to murmur. "They are the fascinating people."

His political work brought Beatty into contact with a great many of these "real stars," putting him on a relaxed footing with the VIPs of the Democratic party. The release of *Shampoo* was widely applauded by the more liberal segment of Washington, D.C.'s elected contingent at the time, and when he was in the capital promoting the movie, he was honored at a luncheon given for him in the Senate dining room by California Senators John Tunney and Alan Cranston. Present at the feast were such luminaries as Hubert Humphrey, Edward Kennedy, Birch Bayh, Jacob Javits, Walter Mondale, Daniel Inouye, and George McGovern. After the meal, Beatty and McGovern sequestered themselves behind closed doors for a private reunion.

The admiration society between Beatty and the politicians was never one-sided. In return for unofficial membership in the select Senate group, Beatty supplied show business glamour.

Senator Gary Hart of Colorado recalls that Warren's relegation to the role of glamour provider for the campaign wasn't exactly what he had planned on when he'd started working for McGovern. Beatty tried to speak on serious issues at the University of Wisconsin in 1971, but the students—who didn't want to hear a movie star's opinions on the world situation—booed him.

After that experience, Beatty told Hart, who was then acting as McGovern's campaign manager, that he didn't want to make any more speaking appearances, but he would think of a way in which he could do his part.

"He invented the political concert," Hart recalls. The biggest of these was held at Madison Square Garden, reuniting groups like Peter, Paul, and Mary and Simon and Garfunkel. With entertainment like that and ushers on the order of Raquel Welch, Paul Newman, Goldie Hawn, and Ryan O'Neal, the show grossed over a quarter of a million dollars.

Later, in 1976, Beatty again displayed his ability to round up a roster of big names when he tossed a private party for Jimmy Carter, then the Democratic party's presidential nominee. Diana Ross, Carroll O'Connor, Faye Dunaway, Lee Grant, and Sidney Poitier were on hand with about fifty other celebrities to greet the candidate from Plains, Georgia at the Beverly Wilshire.

In spite of the lure of Washington, Beatty has always managed to keep both his perspective and his sense of humor where his own political affiliations and ambitions are concerned. When asked how left wing he considered himself, Beatty drily admitted, "Well, I haven't given away what money I have, and at the moment I'm not intending to." Still, he openly admires those politicians he deems worthy of respect, and is pleased with his own contributions to the causes for which he's toiled. After McGovern's humiliating defeat in the Nixon landslide, Warren stated firmly, "I'm *proud* of what I did. It was the right thing to do. If I had to do it over again, there might be a couple of places where I would have changed my approach. I might have tried to use my influence a little differently from the way I did. I learned so much from it that one can't be expected to know that much all at once. But that's private," he added, ending the discussion in his tried and true way, "and I just don't want to go into it."

On a personal level, Beatty viewed his political activities as gratifying in the extreme, but he insisted—and has continued to insist—that he had no plans for running for any office at any time.

"Selfishly, my two years with McGovern were worth it," he

admitted not long after the election results were in. "I gained a great deal of confidence in my currency. When you participate heavily and keep a low profile, you learn. Right now, running myself is unattractive. The silly ego rewards in movies are as great as the ones in politics, but the insults to a movie actor don't approach the insults to a politician. And the level of energy required to do all the compromising is not the same. So . . . as yet, I guess I'm too selfish to run. Also, I'm much more sophisticated about politics than about government and they're two different things."

He has always been aware that his image could hinder him as much as help him were he to seek office. When asked what type of things might hurt him if he were in the public eye as a politician and not movie star, he answered bluntly, "They're sexual." But he quickly added, "And I don't think that sexual things people take very seriously. And as time goes on, people will take them less seriously. Everyone speculates wildly on the sexual habits of others, and most of it is untrue about everybody. If I tried to even keep up with what was said about me sexually, I would be, as Sinatra once said, speaking to you from a jar in the University of Chicago medical center."

But it's not his queasiness about mud slinging that keeps him politically disinclined as much as his queasiness about the political process itself. "I don't know that I have the stomach for it," he has confessed. "There are two different ways of life. The public life of a politician is full of compromises. That's what it's all about—compromises that you know are not exactly right. In movies, you can do more of what you think is right."

For a man who desires, who perhaps actually needs, the greatest degree of control over any project he approaches, the promise of a life of professional compromise is far from appealing. It's for this reason Warren told one acquaintance, "If you ever hear that I'm running for office, you'll know that I've become a much more unselfish person than I am now."

If anything, Warren seems to be heading toward fewer compromises than ever before, taking over as much control as possible on each ensuing project. He sees this—the element of control—as the impetus toward dropping out of acting eventually to concentrate fully on the production end of the business. He says, "One of the most important things about being an actor is to learn how to be out of control; and one of the most important things about being a film-maker is to be able to be in control. There are admirable qualities in being in and out of control, and there's something very vulnerable about allowing yourself to be out of control that does not imply necessarily a lack of discipline or industry; it means a giving in to something. That's necessary to act. I seem to gravitate more toward being in control than out of control, and that is to slip somewhat away from acting."

Beatty has never been secretive about his lust for control. While making *Shampoo*, he confessed, "I enjoy working like this, because I have difficulties when I'm not in control." And, when pressed to reveal his reaction when control is taken from him, he laughed. "I usually get a cold in the second week!"

That desire for control brings its own drawbacks—namely, a tendency to overwork and a need to deal with tiresome details. "I find one problem," Warren once admitted on the subject of making a film his way. "It's not a problem, it's an indulgence. You make a film in your head, and it's pretty good. So you don't want to go to the trouble of actually making it—you don't want to contend with the labs, the unions, the dubbing. It's such a hassle making a film, it's just an industrial task."

And even the compromises required by filmmaking are hard for him to accept. "Politics is constant compromise. Art should never be," he theorizes. "But that prompts a conversation on whether a thing that costs a lot and has a group of people working harrassed schedules should be called art or near-art. It's a hell of a lot easier to see results in movies. I think I'm temperamentally closer to art, but I'm not sure about either. I can say what I have to say in films. In politics, I feel that compromise keeps you from it."

If he were willing to compromise more as a producer, he would be able to delegate more of the production work. But Beatty doesn't want to trust others with even the smallest details. "I used to be more interested in making money," he admitted while filming *Shampoo*, "but when you have as much as I do, what really matters is to do exactly what you want as an artist."

To do that, he personally oversees every task on his films, becoming a virtual recluse who has time for nothing else but the movie being made. "I'm living in my dressing room," he said matter-of-factly during the making of *Shampoo*, "because why take the time to drive home, read *The New York Times*, and return? When I'm acting in a movie, I go out at night, but producing is a whole other thing. I'd miss the night life if the film lasted for seven or eight months. We've only got sixty days."

That mania, that drive to get what he wants in a motion picture, has impressed everyone who has worked with Beatty in his capacity as producer. Richard Sylbert, set designer for *Reds*, also worked for Warren on *Shampoo*. He has said, "He's a great producer. He's very strong and devoted to the idea. They threw him out of every studio on *Bonnie*, as they did with this film, but he's not a bumbler or a hustler. He's a tough negotiator. He asks for a lot and gets it."

Buck Henry, who co-directed *Heaven Can Wait* with Beatty, was awestruck by Warren's insistence on involving himself in almost every aspect of the picture's production. "He likes to work under pressure," Henry revealed, "and if it's not there, he'll create it. He's a demonic producer. . . . He fills every minute. Nothing deters him, nothing stops him. He barely sleeps, and he likes to do as much as possible himself."

Warren's attention to detail, in Henry's opinion, threatens to burn him out by the time a film is completed. "Beatty is psychotic about the possibility of overlooking anything," he said emphatically after working side by side with Warren on *Heaven Can Wait*. "If he could, he would be up in the projection booth of the theater showing his movie, pushing the projectionist aside, still trying to cut or add frames, humming music he might have forgotten to include in the sound track. 'Easygoing' is not a quality he has. You know how presidents age in office? If Beatty were president, either he would be dead after the first year or the country would be dead, because his attention to detail is maniacal."

His zeal as a producer has flabbergasted even those who thought they knew him well before working with him. One of these is writer Jerzy Kosinski, who, after appearing in *Reds*, confessed in astonishment, "I have known Warren since 1968. But it was only when I worked on *Reds* that I suddenly realized how little I knew him. From seven-thirty in the morning until twelve-thirty at night, he was absolutely in control. There were moments so astounding that I felt if Chrysler had been run by Warren Beatty, it would never have suffered a loss."

Rona Barrett, who knows practically everything there is to know about everybody and who has known Warren since those lean days in New York, summed up the situation this way: "I see him now and then and it's always warm and very friendly. I love Warren, but I think he's a whore. He's very spoiled and selfish. He only does what he wants to do when he wants to do it. He was that way when he was poor and he's that way now. He'll run his rear end off promoting a picture if it's his movie, but if he's doing a picture for somebody else, he couldn't care less. He hasn't changed, and I don't think he ever will."

When it *is* his movie, he can be tireless when promotion time rolls around. He hyped *Shampoo* across the country, even entertaining the foreign press with an eye toward the Golden Globe Award. He was determined that it not have the acceptance problems *Bonnie and Clyde* had encountered on its initial release. As he told one reporter, "You would laugh if you read the early reviews of *Bonnie and Clyde*. They all said it's impermissible, you can't do this, you can't put that kind of music with that kind of film, you can't have those cops reacting to those things, you can't have comedy and violence juxtaposed, you can't do that, it's all a failure, it doesn't work, the actors are all buffoons and clowns, who're they trying to kid, we can't take these people seriously. All kinds of rather interesting criticism.

"What I try to do is not have any rearview-mirror thinking

govern the decisions that are made with a film. And it relates to the publicity that has been created around certain people. So it really becomes some con job to try to give a film a fair shake."

Warren was motivated to promote *Shampoo* even more vigorously because he feared his main character would be misunderstood. He verbalized a great deal in defense of George and *Shampoo* in general.

"The college kids understand it," he said of the movie. "They have a greater tolerance for multiple sex. The monogamous ideal is not laughed at by these people, but they know you can have multiple sex experiences and not be depressed by the Victorian and Freudian rules that are disobeyed. Freud had not patience with promiscuity. Freud would *not* have laughed at this picture."

So unstinting was he in support of George's sexual proclivities that *Shampoo* was viewed (and reviewed) by many as Warren Beatty's defense of his own sexuality, a charge he encouraged rather than denied. "I've always tried to keep my private life private," he said, as he has said before. Only, this time around, there was a new addendum. "But I've read what people say about me. If they want to think of me as a sex object, that's fine. I think I'd be worried if they didn't!"

And, in defense of promiscuity, he pontificated, "There seems to be a specific need to say in a Puritan-based society that if a character indulges in something that is not monogamy, he will eventually find the light. If he doesn't, he'll be punished. I don't participate in that kind of moralizing. I would just say it takes more energy to be promiscuous. It makes concentration difficult, and one has a tendency not to get much work done. But I didn't mean to be negative about nonmonogamous sex. I think it can be a lot of fun; but so can monogamy."

What is missing from this statement is any indication that one's emotions or spirituality play any part in the sexual experience. Rarely did Beatty ever bring up the notion of love when discussing sexuality in terms of *Shampoo*.

Interestingly enough, Beatty did see George as a victim of his own sexual drives, a condition he applied to males in general, and which he referred to as an important difference between men (himself included) and women, saying, "Well, I think I've always treated women as equals. But I think men are more controlled by their libidos—although it's going to be different in the future. In the past, we thought we could deal with the outer limits of male sexuality. We're getting into an era where male and female sexuality are treated equally and I think we're going to discover those outer limits of female sexuality just may be further out. As society moves further away from keeping the female enslaved, it opens up the possibilities of the adventurous woman investigating her outer limits, and I think she may become as victimized by her libido as the male."

Thus far, that prediction hasn't come true. Perhaps not enough time has passed for women to delve into those "outer limits," or perhaps women have always been more in touch emotionally with the high price paid for promiscuity—not in terms of self-respect or the judgments of a puritanical society, but in terms of human loneliness and the emptiness that accompanies the so-called swinging lifestyle, where other people are viewed as objects to be used for pleasure and then discarded.

To a degree, Beatty appeared to have missed the point of George's relation to the opposite sex. He saw George as a man who loved women, was basically kind if slovenly, had a load of guilt left over from childhood, was not latently homosexual, and had no hostility toward women. Never once did he mention the stark terror of emotional involvement that seems to propel George through the entirety of *Shampoo*. Instead of viewing George as an immature womanizer who seeks sensation to compensate for his lack of depth, and who can give little to women other than his body, Beatty saw him as "ahead of his time."

In the long run, of course, the philosophy behind *Shampoo* was not as important as the fact that it's an entertaining, well-made motion picture. Warren's enthusiasm for certain projects may be morally ignited, but audiences are drawn not by the philosophical premises engendered in a movie, which are strikingly naive for a man of Beatty's sophistication, but by the action of the story.

Beatty can explain that "the subject of violence and its socio-economic root causes and the casualizing of violence was stimulating enough for me to stick with *Bonnie and Clyde* . . ." or that "the sexual revolution of the sixties was stimulating enough for me to do *Shampoo* . . ." but neither of these considerations affected the average moviegoer, who was there simply to be entertained.

And it is here that Warren Beatty's ultimate gift as a producer rests. In spite of his contention that one has to "kind of earn the right to produce a movie on a certain subject," he has produced entertaining films on inherently serious subjects. The film he produced after *Shampoo* is no exception. With *Heaven Can Wait*, Beatty turned his attention to concocting a frothy, lighthearted motion picture about human mortality, something generally considered no laughing matter.

Warren Beatty dazzled audiences in his first movie, *Splendor in the Grass*.
Pictorial Parade

RIGHT: Warren Beatty and Joan Collins donned western garb for the Hollywood premiere of *The Alamo*. Pictorial Parade

BELOW: This still from *Lilith* doesn't reflect the tension that existed among Peter Fonda, Jean Seberg, and Warren Beatty. United Press International

ABOVE: Beatty escorts Joan Collins to the premiere of *Can-Can*. Jack Albin, Pictorial Parade

LEFT: The making of *Splendor in the Grass* saw romance blossom between Beatty and his co-star, Natalie Wood. Here the two are seen en route to the Cannes Film Festival. Pictorial Parade

During his love affair with Leslie Caron, Beatty placed their romance above his own career considerations. They never made it to the altar, though. Frank Edwards Fotos International

Beatty was gambling with his career when he chose to produce *Bonnie and Clyde*, but the gamble paid off. Here Beatty and his co-star Faye Dunaway are shown during their trip to Paris for the movie's French premiere. Pictorial Parade

Julie Christie and Beatty have remained close friends although their romance is over.
Frank Edwards Fotos International

Warren Beatty and sister, Shirley MacLaine, sign autographs during Senator George McGovern's presidential campaign in 1972. Brian Hamill, Photoreporters

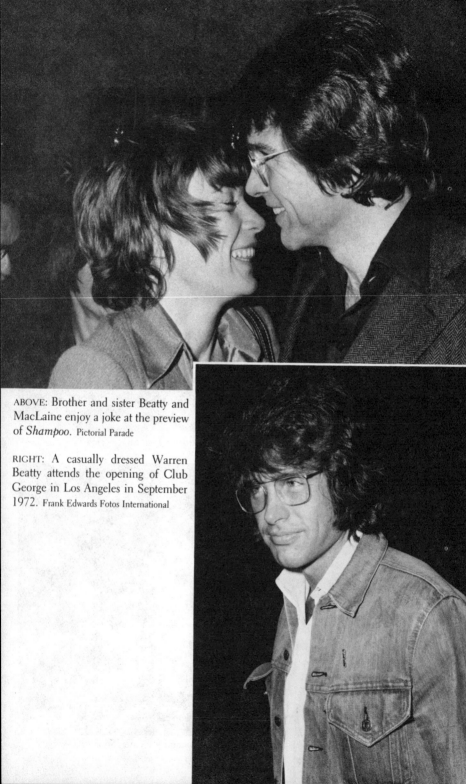

ABOVE: Brother and sister Beatty and MacLaine enjoy a joke at the preview of *Shampoo*. Pictorial Parade

RIGHT: A casually dressed Warren Beatty attends the opening of Club George in Los Angeles in September 1972. Frank Edwards Fotos International

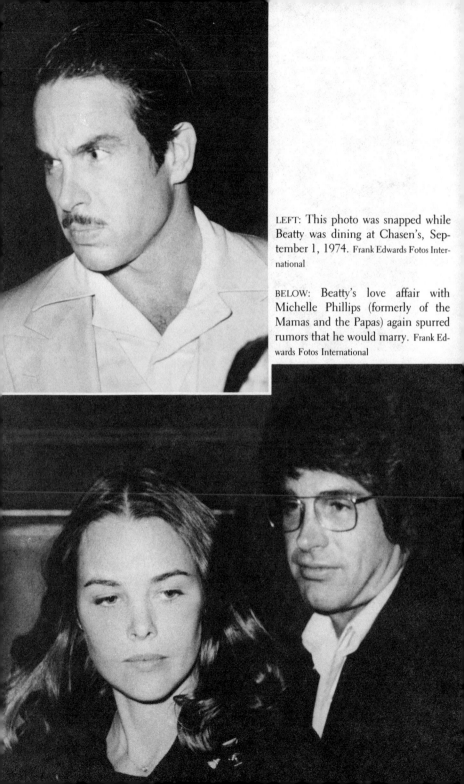

LEFT: This photo was snapped while Beatty was dining at Chasen's, September 1, 1974. Frank Edwards Fotos International

BELOW: Beatty's love affair with Michelle Phillips (formerly of the Mamas and the Papas) again spurred rumors that he would marry. Frank Edwards Fotos International

ABOVE: Beatty and Diane Keaton were a twosome at the Academy Awards ceremony in 1979. Frank Edwards Fotos International

RIGHT: Beatty and model Dale Haddon were deep in conversation when this photo was taken. Photoreporters

ABOVE: Diane Keaton and Warren Beatty in a scene from *Reds*. United Press International Photo

LEFT: The family resemblance is strong in this picture of Warren Beatty and Shirley MacLaine.

BELOW: Beatty shares a table with Jerzy Kosinski at the New York Film Critics Awards. Tom Gates, Pictorial Parade

A proud Warren Beatty holds his Oscar for Best Director, awarded for *Reds*. Frank Edwards Fotos International

Co-stars Diane Keaton a Warren Beatty arrive for t Fifty-fourth Academy Awa in March 1982. United Press ternational Photo

13

HEAVEN CAN WAIT: TACKLING IMMORTALITY

Before tackling *Heaven Can Wait*, Beatty had one more picture to do for someone else. *The Fortune*, directed by his friend Mike Nichols, teamed him with another friend, one of his closest buddies, Jack Nicholson.

In a takeoff on the madcap comedies of the thirties, Warren and Jack played two idiotic lounge lizards determined to bilk sanitary napkin heiress Stockard Channing out of her fortune. The movie flopped at the box office, though much of it is actually uproariously funny. Beatty's performance is a small gem, as he mugs and chews up the scenery, more than holding his own against notorious scene stealer Nicholson. With his slicked-down hair and pencil-thin mustache, Beatty's character could be the eccentric twin to the gigolo he played in *The Roman Spring of Mrs. Stone* (though some might insist he was funnier with the Italian accent).

In his last films as an actor directed by others, Beatty got along splendidly with his directors. The opinionated youngster who walked all over directors if given half a chance was gone. When asked at this time if, as an actor, he preferred a director whom he could direct, Beatty quickly said, "Oh, no. When I'm a hired actor, I really much prefer someone who's in very firm command of his film, if he's any good. It's just much easier."

Beatty had two projects on his agenda for consideration after *The Fortune*: one, the story of John Reed, which would finally emerge as *Reds*; the other, a remake of a popular old comedy that would be reincarnated as *Heaven Can Wait*. As he promoted

Shampoo around the country, he wasn't yet sure which project he would attack first, or if he would direct his next film.

"I don't know," he answered when asked if he would soon be directing a movie himself. "It's a funny mechanism. When I prepare a movie—this happened on both movies that I produced, *Bonnie and Clyde* and *Shampoo*—I get to a certain point in the picture and I say, 'The truth is that this material will be better served by having an additional eye watching our work, so I should try to arrange that.' The question is whether the extra opinion that you gain by having a director direct you is valuable enough to make up for the amount of energy that's expended in diplomacy, in working that relationship out in a film. In these two films, the answer for me was yes."

By the time he made *Shampoo*, Warren was getting increasingly closer to taking on the mantle of director himself, stating, "I'm not a hired actor in *Shampoo*. I knew very firmly what I wanted. I don't mean to demean what anyone else wanted, Hal Ashby or Robert Towne, but we acted in concert, and I don't feel there was any separation of what we wanted."

As a producer, of course, Beatty could point a director on the tack he wished to take with much more authority than he ever could have as a hired actor. When the cast of *Shampoo* was rehearsing one scene set in the salon where George worked, Beatty took command, telling Ashby he didn't want to use the hair blower to dry George's pretty client's hair because it would make too much noise. "I'll show you how I see this scene," he told the director. Then he straddled his legs over the girl's lap, pushed her head forward toward his crotch, and began massaging her scalp as he joked, "I want this to be a totally asexual scene." Needless to say, that scene was in the finished movie just as Warren had envisioned it.

Besides planning *Heaven Can Wait* and *Reds*, Beatty had another future project in mind, one still in the embryonic stages, a film biography of Howard Hughes. Beatty was more intensely drawn toward the two movies based on real people, but he was well aware the material of both was more problematical than that embodied in a gentle comedy. "They are difficult productions that I would like to direct myself," he admitted. "So I decided I better direct something more simple first. So I decided to make a movie that I would enjoy seeing. That's why I made *Heaven Can Wait*."

The original movie, entitled *Here Comes Mr. Jordan*, was a big hit when it was released in 1941 with Robert Montgomery and Claude Rains as its stars. It was later remade, not as successfully, as *Down to Earth* in 1947, with Rita Hayworth as the star attraction.

Beatty was looking for "a nice yarn with a strong narrative" when he happened upon *Here Comes Mr. Jordan*. He was immediately drawn to the story.

". . . I kept returning to the idea of a romantic fantasy," he explained, "because that's what *I* wanted to see. Maybe I was even a little depressed at the time. A couple of my friends had died. Something about the size of the theme didn't seem small. It was dealing with death and reincarnation. That made me want to see it particularly.

"I wanted to do something that would be very clear, very clean, something unashamedly linear where I wouldn't be able to indulge myself too much. The demands of that particular form are so clear you don't have much chance to be. It's like walking a tightrope because the transparency of your intentions is so easily derided.

"But it was an attempt to fulfill one of the valid functions of the theater, which is to entertain and make you feel better if we can."

The hero of the original *Here Comes Mr. Jordan* was a boxer, so Beatty first approached his friend Muhammad Ali about taking on the role. The fighter was interested, but fighting came first and he had some matches on his schedule, so it would have been impossible for him to consider the offer seriously. Luckily, Beatty had a backup actor for the role—himself.

"I couldn't see myself as a boxer," he said, explaining a major difference between *Here Comes Mr. Jordan* and *Heaven Can Wait*, "but I had been a football player as a kid. So I changed it."

Beatty went to Elaine May for the screenplay, which he co-wrote. Then he had two grueling chores to face: casting the other roles in the film and getting himself in shape to play quarterback after about a quarter of a century off the football field. He approached his athletic training with the same diligence he exhibits where any facet of his filmmaking is concerned. By the time the cameras were ready to roll, Beatty was in superb physical condition.

After considering both Cary Grant and former Senator Eugene McCarthy (one of Beatty's political coterie) for the role of Mr. Jordan, the heavenly bureaucrat, Beatty signed James Mason, whose voice has always carried such authority it might have been granted by His dispensation. Once again he "promoted" Julie Christie into co-starring opposite him, with co-director Buck Henry playing Mr. Jordan's ineptly angelic assistant, Dyan Cannon and Charles Grodin as a duo with murder on their minds, Jack Warden as a trainer, and Dolph Sweet, a coach. To top off the star-studded cast, Beatty hired several Los Angeles Rams to play Rams and some professional sportscasters to portray themselves.

In the beginning, Beatty had no intention of getting involved in the film's direction. "I asked Mike [Nichols] and Arthur [Penn]," he admitted, "but they were busy. Then I thought the next best thing would be to do it myself."

Ever cautious, Beatty decided not to take the plunge solo, and he contracted Buck Henry to take on the job of co-director. Henry found acting in the movie a less demanding job than that of co-director, and he said afterward, "We had plenty of disagreements, but they weren't violent. When Warren wants to do something his way, he has it all figured out. So you goddamn well better be prepared to argue your case if you differ with him."

Arguments or not, *Heaven Can Wait* was a rousing success, having earned $77 million at the box office thus far. The movie also earned even greater respect for Warren Beatty as a producer, the general consensus being that bringing out a whimsical romantic comedy in 1978 was a risky proposition indeed.

The producer didn't agree with that theory, insisting, "It seemed to me no risk at all. It was a movie that I wanted to see. I thought something that was clean and funny and romantic would be a good way to spend an hour and a half. The problem with *me* was that I had to spend a year and a half to make it, and that's a lot of work. You lose your judgment during the editing process and you get so sick of *looking* at yourself."

Once again, Beatty's judgment of what the public wanted paid off. *Bonnie and Clyde* addressed itself to audiences hungry for anti-heroes, *Shampoo* geared itself to a society in the midst of a major sexual revolution, and *Heaven Can Wait* offered whole-hearted entertainment for the millions who had found violence and tragedy too close to their front doors to seek it on the movie screens.

The plot is, as its producer has said, linear and straightforward. Beatty plays Joe Pendleton, a quarterback for the Los Angeles Rams, who is summoned to heaven before his time after a bike-truck collision in the Mulholland Tunnel. He insists on going back to earth, and reappears as a tycoon marked for murder by his wife and her lover. Joe Pendleton, not about to allow the assumption of a new identity to upset his plans, trains for the Super Bowl, buys the Rams, and wins the game, with a heart-tugging romance with Julie Christie along the way, before he at last boards a Concorde for his return to heaven.

Frank Rich, writing for *Time*, was enthusiastic, pointing out that *Heaven Can Wait* ". . . has everything going for it: big laughs, populist politics, billowy sequences set in heaven, a murder plot, a climactic Super Bowl game, a supporting cast of choice comic actors . . . and, best of all, a touching (but P.G.) romance between the hero and co-star Julie Christie, who communicate largely through passionate eye contact."

The majority of the nation's reviewers agreed. Rather than attacking Beatty for his frothy concoction, most, like the *Los Angeles Times*' Charles Champlin, saw *Heaven Can Wait* as a step in the right direction.

"What *Heaven Can Wait* preserves and presents," said Champlin in his laudatory review, "is a wonderful innocence—funny, lyrically romantic and optimistic. It is as buoyantly cheerful as Beatty's *Shampoo* was scathingly and depressingly sardonic and cynical." And he credited the star's "likable boyish charm" with sustaining the movie.

Beatty knew his motion picture had the unbeatable elements that would make it a crowd-pleaser. He also knew that, more important, it had a moral to gratify every moviegoer. "Hey, let's face it," he remarked, "the movie says you're not going to die."

Heaven Can Wait remains a fluke in Beatty's roster of productions, the only film he has made that's embraced anything close to sunny optimism. *Reds* stands a study in bleakness and futility, and one cannot imagine that the story of Howard Hughes can contain more light than shadow.

And yet, *Heaven Can Wait* does concern a very serious subject, death, not an unusual choice of topic for a filmmaker who turned forty the·year it was made. After he made *Shampoo*, a reflective Beatty confessed, ". . . I think there's a moment in time when you stay up too late and wake up the next morning saying, 'God, I really am older.'" *Heaven Can Wait* is the work of a man who wakes up one morning and realizes, "God, I really am not going to live forever." Because of that, the film soothes an anxiety, omnipresent if subconscious, of the entire human race.

Beatty was now firmly established as a successful producer. And when anyone referred to him simply as an actor, he was quick to correct them. "I don't think of myself as an actor," he reminded folks. "I think an actor acts. Albert Finney is an actor, he acts all the time. I act, I produce, I'll try to write something, I'll be a politician . . . I'm a sometimes actor, an unconcentrated actor."

As a producer, he was more comfortable in interviews. Now, though he still disliked discussing individual films, he could wax eloquent on the filmmaking process, a field in which he labored long hours to gain the right to refer to himself as a filmmaker. He enjoyed his work on the other side of the camera, because it freed him from what he'd always considered an unnaturally narcissistic position. "In an interview situation," he once complained, "especially the show business interview, you're being asked, 'What do you think of yourself?' 'How do you think you look?' 'What do you think people think of you?' 'What do you want to show about yourself?' That's why it's so much easier to do political interviews, because they're really about something else. If you do a personal film, people say, 'Why is this personal to you?' Well: I, I, I, I, I, I, I. So, of course that forces you into a narcissistic stance. If you're fast on your feet, you can try to get out of it. Films itself do that [sic], making films."

The three films he had produced brought him more than self-respect and the respect of the film community—it has been estimated that his share of the profits of *Bonnie and Clyde, Shampoo,* and *Heaven Can Wait* have netted him approximately $100 million—enough, as one critic pointed out, to enable him to finance the entirety of *Reds* himself.

With *Heaven Can Wait* a solid smash, Beatty was in no hurry to rush into anything new. Now he had time to contemplate *Reds,* the biographical movie based on John Reed's *Ten Days That Shook the World.* And there was no question about his rushing into that, since as far back as 1971 he confessed of that project, "One thing that's holding it up is my own inertia."

With no money problems and a project dear to his heart progressing at its own snail-like pace, Beatty could take a break and turn back to the good life he has always enjoyed so much. In the three years it took *Reds* to hit the screen after the release of *Heaven Can Wait,* Warren Beatty wasn't forgotten. But his publicity value remained constant because of his romances, not because he agreed to appear in anyone else's motion picture. As he himself said, "Making a lot of movies is a waste of time. I'd rather waste it in the conventional way."

14

THE SOLID CITIZEN
OF THE SEVENTIES

In 1976, while talking to Alan Ebert on the subject of Warren Beatty (for an article that appeared in *Ladies' Home Journal*), Beatty's *Shampoo* co-writer Robert Towne said, "In the ten years I've known Warren, I haven't seen him lose his interest in women and doubt if I *ever* will. When you are excessively handsome *and* charming *and* witty *and* intelligent, the opportunities are vast. In Warren's case, they are greater than any other man's times ten! And he takes advantage of them."

In 1975, it once again seemed that Warren had found the woman to make him give up his wandering ways. Unlike his other serious love interests, Michelle Phillips is not petite. Nor is she voluptuous à la Joan Collins, demure as was the young Natalie Wood, possessed of Leslie Caron's gamine quality, or down-to-earth and tomboyish like Julie Christie. Carrying a scant hundred pounds on her five-foot-seven frame, Michelle was the perfect match for Beatty's new sophistication. Bone thin, with finely chiseled features, honey-blond hair, and a stylish designer wardrobe, Phillips was the ideal companion for the New Hollywood.

By the time she hooked up with Warren, Michelle had acquired a degree of elegance compatible with having hopped straight from the social register into Hollywood. In actuality, she was the daughter of a seaman (her mother died when Michelle was a young child), who married singer/songwriter John Phillips while she was still in her teens.

Together with Cass Elliot and Denny Doherty, John and

Michelle Phillips were the Mamas and the Papas, one of the most popular singing groups of the Monterey Pop generation, famous for songs like "Monday, Monday," "Creeque Alley" and "California Dreamin'."

The marriage produced one child, a daughter named China, now in her teens, but the breakup of John and Michelle occurred around the same time the Mamas and Papas broke up.

Instead of staying with singing, Michelle took up acting—and actors. A quickie marriage to actor Dennis (*Easy Rider*) Hopper lasted only a matter of weeks. Shortly after that union was dissolved, romance bloomed between Michelle and Hopper's close friend (and another *Easy Rider* cast member), Jack Nicholson.

Michelle and Nicholson spent two years together, with Nicholson even acquiring the house next door to his on Mulholland Drive for Michelle and her daughter when Michelle decided she didn't want to rush into living *with* him. However, separate domiciles didn't seem to be the answer, because just when their friends were expecting a wedding announcement, they instead received the news that Michelle and Jack had split.

In the clannish, incestuous style that has become synonymous with the so-called New Hollywood, Michelle went from Jack to his closest friend. Not only did this cause no hard feelings on Nicholson's part—he had Warren and Michelle to his Aspen, Colorado house for Christmas in 1975—but the whole gang remained on the best of terms. Warren and Michelle frequently dined with John Phillips and his then wife, Genevieve Waite (who had been the star of the ill-fated *Joanna*, produced by Leslie Caron's then-husband Michael Laughlin).

Beatty gradually had been drifting toward a more settled lifestyle than ever before. He was now close to forty; it would have surprised none of his friends if he were to announce an impending marriage.

Even during his days with Julie Christie, Warren hadn't seemed as put off by the settled-down aspects of marriage as by the fact of marriage itself. "Julie and I haven't lived so differently from married people," he insisted. "We just haven't married. People nowadays expect to go from one marriage to another. Humans change. Society should not be surprised. Is it fair to take a woman and make the vows one makes in a marriage ceremony and then wink at them, saying, 'We always knew we could get out of it?'"

In 1974, he prided himself on his lack of possessions as much as on the absence of permanent personal ties, telling Joan Dew, "I bought a car this year for the first time since I've lived in Hollywood. That, my books and records, and a few clothes are all I own. I like to feel that if I take off for London tomorrow, I won't be leaving anything behind." With a gesture around his small Beverly Wilshire suite, he went on, "This is really all I need. Besides, being here is convenient."

He preferred, he explained time and again, being able to "rent everything." What he couldn't rent, he bought, then stored in warehouses. Until giving in and buying a car, he rented those as well, usually black Cadillacs or Mercedes. Besides a sparse wardrobe of casual clothes, his closets at the Beverly Wilshire held only four suits and one dinner jacket. He shunned stability of residence as fervently as he avoided monogamy.

"We move in a time when tranquilizers, polygamy, so many alternatives are offered to working out the difficulties of a marriage," he once sighed pessimistically. "This business of you go with a person, you live with a person, you marry a person, you divorce a person—there is no substitute for the particular depth that is provided by time. Why don't you ask about the value of monogamy and the genius it requires?"

As Julie Christie had denied she possessed the "talent" for marriage, so it seemed Warren lacked the "genius" necessary for monogamy—and even the knack required to set up housekeeping by himself.

He bought a house when he was in love with Julie Christie, but, after they split up, he never got around to moving into it, preferring isolation at the top of the Beverly Wilshire to being isolated in a huge house in a secluded canyon. But once Michelle had entered his life, he threw himself wholeheartedly into the role of homeowner, hiring decorators and preparing his abode for residence.

Mulholland Drive has long been one of the choice living areas in Los Angeles, a high mountain road overlooking the city and connecting the various canyons (Laurel, Benedict, Coldwater, Beverly Glen) that cut through the San Fernando Valley and lead to Hollywood. Beatty's house, the former Lauritz Melchior estate, sits in several acres of grounds, lush with fruit trees and flowering plants, down the road from his friend Jack Nicholson's place and a brief ten-minute drive from Beverly Hills or Hollywood.

The house, an older one, is constructed along typically California lines. Open and airy, it boasts a great deal of glass and gleaming white walls. There is a sizable swimming pool, as well as a manmade lagoon and jacuzzi, and Warren had the tennis court resurfaced before moving in.

The rooms are simply, almost starkly, furnished, in keeping with the personality of a man who wants a "no frills" mode of existence. But amenities are not lacking. There's a giant color television screen and projection area, and an enormous freezer well stocked with the lord of the manor's favorite ice-cream flavors.

When Beatty moved into the house with Phillips, he did so in a tentative, exploratory manner, retaining his suite at the hotel while she, too, rented an apartment of her own. Today, the house continues to give off an unlived-in feeling. Instead of becoming a permanent home for its owner, it's been relegated to existing as yet another way station in a frenetic and nomadic existence.

With Michelle and China, Warren spent a great many hours in the house and around the pool. He basked in his ready-made family, even driving China to school mornings in his new unrented car, a tobacco brown Mercedes Benz 450 SL sedan.

Self-acceptance had brought with it a new appreciation of stability. Though still adamant in his flight from boredom, Beatty now confessed that ". . . a lot of things that seemed exciting to me five years ago aren't exciting to me now."

Diminished self-involvement had brought with it an increased interest in the world at large, an interest fostered by his political involvement. Wealth and power supplied freedom and also called for added responsibility. Though he's never flaunted his wealth, Warren had now entered the world of high finance. As a producer and a millionaire, he was required to keep abreast of trends in commerce.

"I certainly have no guilt feelings about it," he said of his wealth, "and I'm not victimized. I like to think that the people I choose after some careful scrutiny will look after my interests. I have a business manager. I have some interest in business, but I'm more interested in what the market is doing in general—what overall changes are coming—than in what happens to a particular stock."

From the time he produced *Bonnie and Clyde*, Beatty had been undergoing a gradual yet major change. He was still ambitious, but with a significant success as a producer under his belt at the age of thirty, he was no longer as driven as he had been. As he himself put it, he ". . . sort of relaxed and thought, well, what am I really running after? Why don't I just have some fun and do some studying and some living? I really picked up more interest in politics and economics. . . ."

Along the way, he picked up more rational living habits as well. Never a big smoker or drinker, he's content with a puff of someone else's cigarette (when he does smoke a whole cigarette, he refrains from inhaling) and an occasional glass of wine. The junk food he had survived on as a young actor was given up, not only because of his newfound wealth, but also because of a raised consciousness. In 1970, he revealed, "I find myself turning more and more to organically grown foods. Some people think that's silly, but only a few years ago they called Rachel Carson a crazy lady for writing a book about the balance of nature. And only a few years ago, they said everyone was crazy for worrying about DDT. Now even the Republicans fear it," he added, never one to leave anyone in doubt about his political sympathies.

If his aversion to alcohol was an anomaly in the hedonistic

world of the New Hollywood, Beatty's attitude toward recreational drugs was downright reactionary, especially when one considers that his friends included admitted potheads and that life in the fast lane, show-business style, has exalted cocaine snorting to a status approaching religious fervor. Warren's conservatism in this area is genuine. Not only has there never been even a breath of rumor about his tooting a line or two of white powder, he's even gone on record as stating that the drug problem is "one of the most serious we're facing today," and even at the risk of being thought uptight, he mulishly asserts, ". . . It hasn't been proven to me yet that marijuana does not cause chromosomal or brain damage."

In the mid seventies, Beatty pursued a relatively conservative lifestyle. His sole vice, other than a tendency to push himself too hard, seemed to be women, and Michelle Phillips was doing her best to turn that into a virtue, icily informing one female reporter with whom Warren was flirting, "He likes monogamy just fine."

For a celebrated womanizer, Beatty genuinely does seem to lean toward monogamy, paradoxical though this may sound. On the one hand, he spent the seventies romancing such disparate women as Liv Ullmann, Britt Ekland, Joni Mitchell, Maya Plisetskaya and Carly Simon (Beatty is supposed to be the subject of her scathing "You're So Vain"). On the other, he appeared happiest during this decade when he concentrated on one woman at a time; first, Julie Christie, and then Michelle Phillips. One could say that by nature Beatty is monogamous, while by choice he disdains remaining faithful.

A one-woman man (again and again and again), Warren finds the end of any relationship inherent in its beginning. Unlike those who think nothing of making vows "till death do us part," Beatty views the initiation of intimacies as the first step toward their termination. "The best time to get married is noon," he once joked. "That way if things don't work out, you haven't blown the whole day."

Beatty himself has even compared marriage to another kind of contract, saying, "Marriage is like the old seven-year studio contract;

it's fallen on hard times. That has nothing to do with romance or love, though. They exist without it. I like to think that I picked up on living with people ten years before it happened."

If the marriage contract is anathema to Beatty, the married way of life is not. He likes long-term relationships; he likes to live with the women he loves. But when the pressure is on to prod him toward the altar, domestic bliss quickly fades.

And so Michelle Phillips joined the roster of women who have not become Mrs. Warren Beatty, moving out of Warren's spread on Mulholland and into her own apartment on a full-time basis. With the breakup of their romance, Michelle threw herself wholeheartedly into furthering her acting career while Beatty once again focused his full attention on the project at hand.

Though he blamed his own inertia for stalling off active production on the John Reed story, Beatty had never let the saga of the leftist journalist stray from his mind. From the start, he had identified with Reed, and the more he came to terms with his own ambition, the more Beatty became obsessed with Reed's life.

Warren has always felt it necessary to "earn the right" to produce any film, the prime case being *Shampoo*, where he laughingly admitted his right was earned by his own reputation. His interest in politics and the personal questions raised by that interest now fired his opinion that he had earned the right to produce a film about John Reed, bolstered by his assertion that he knew as much about Reed as anyone else. He approached the production not only as a producer trying to say something or tell a story this time, but as a man on a quest, seeking answers to his own questions. What he wished to confront through the life of Reed, he told one interviewer, was the "abdication of your personal life for a political life and whether it's fruitful, and if it is, how fruitful is it? How much do you have to give up?"

When he made that statement, he was not yet aware how much he would give up to immerse himself in Reed's past, how consumed he would be by the task of bringing a segment of that past to the screen.

15

PLAYBOY OF THE
SOCIAL REVOLUTION

Who was John Reed? The scion of a wealthy family, he was born in Portland, Oregon, in 1887 and educated at Harvard. By the time he left Cambridge, his leftist sympathies were firmly entrenched as was his journalistic vocation. After settling in Greenwich Village in Manhattan, he became a regular contributor to *The Masses*, editor Max Eastman's left-wing activist publication. Reed quickly established his specialty: on-the-spot reporting, first covering a momentous silk mill strike in Paterson, New Jersey, then journeying to Mexico to write firsthand commentary on Pancho Villa's insurrection.

Thanks to his exciting stories filed while riding side by side with the Mexican bandits, Reed was already considered a great journalist when he went to Russia in 1917, having been told that "big things" were about to happen there. Arriving in Petrograd in time to witness the uprising of the Bolsheviks and the birth of the Russian Revolution, he vividly recounted his experiences in his best-known literary effort, *Ten Days That Shook the World*. He succumbed to typhus and died in Moscow on October 17, 1920, five days before his thirty-third birthday. John Reed is the only American buried within the Kremlin walls.

Warren Beatty might have been born to play Reed, whom fellow writer (*The Jungle*) and activist Upton Sinclair nicknamed "the playboy of the social revolution."

"Every act of rebelling," the French writer and philosopher Albert Camus wrote, "expresses a nostalgia for innocence." That same nostalgia lured Reed to the strikes, the insurrections, the up-heavals and revolutions. He wanted to be there when the rebellions took place, for he was, as Robert A. Rosenstone notes in *Romantic Revolutionary*, his biography of Reed, a man who "never wholly abandoned boyhood dreams of an epic life."

Warren Beatty became enamored of the romantic whom historian Bertram D. Wolfe described, among other things, as "perpetually immature," while vacationing in the Soviet Union during the sixties. There he made the acquaintance of a woman who had been Reed's lover. The seeds of an idea for the future were planted, and not long afterward, Beatty began studying the Russian language.

After his first trip to the Soviet Union (with Natalie Wood when they were lovers—she was of Russian heritage), he returned several more times. He also romanced Russian émigrée Maya Plisetskaya, who gave him a special insight into the land and its people.

Beatty's research was diligent and time-consuming. At Harvard's Widener Memorial Library, he pored over the John Reed archives. On his own, he studied other sources for background on the Bolsheviks and the revolution of 1917. Unable to handle by himself the massive amount of research he deemed necessary, he hired researchers to provide him with background on the political radicalism and left-wing presses of the early twentieth century. He ran ads in various publications, seeking any of Reed's contemporaries still living and willing to talk to him.

As far back as 1972, Beatty was in contact with people who had known Reed, filming the first of many "witness" interviews with Manny Kamrov, an old-time New York leftist. Of the thirty-two witnesses who appear onscreen in *Reds*, several, including writers Henry Miller and Will Durant, had died by the time the film was released. Many of the interviews filmed by cinematographer Vittorio Storaro didn't survive the final cutting stage; some of the individual interviews ran for up to two hours.

All of this took place over a period of years. But then, Beatty had earned the money and the right to work at his own pace. *Reds* would be his sixteenth motion picture after more than twenty years in Hollywood.

The esteemed British playwright Trevor Griffiths was hired to write the screenplay, Beatty having been impressed by Griffiths' scathing portrayal of unofficial class warfare in his stage play *The Comedians*, which had been a hit both in London and, later, on Broadway. The bulk of this script would later be discarded when Beatty decided Griffiths had played up the political angle to the detriment of the romantic. Politics may rule Warren's heart, but his head is astute enough to realize that it would be the love affair between Reed and Louise Bryant that would bring in the movie-goers and the money.

Most of the finished script was the work of Beatty himself, though he also had his *Heaven Can Wait* co-writer Elaine May shuttling back and forth between Europe and New York to help him with revisions, and he was also assisted in the rewriting by *Shampoo*'s Robert Towne. The script was still being revised while the cameras were rolling.

Beatty had considered directing *Reds* himself; it was with an eye to this that he co-directed *Heaven Can Wait* with Buck Henry. Directing had long been one of his goals, but for one reason or another he kept putting it off, explaining in the mid seventies, "I was going to direct *Bonnie and Clyde*, and I almost directed *Shampoo*. But in both situations I felt it would be fairer to the material to get someone in who had a fresh eye. The same thing could happen with the John Reed story—or maybe I *will* wind up directing this one myself."

With *Reds*, Beatty finally felt ready to direct on his own. Besides, on this production, the most important of his life, he wanted, he demanded, total control.

Edward Herrmann, who plays Max Eastman in *Reds*, made an insightful comment after the movie was completed. What he said of Reed could easily be applied to Beatty: "To be serious about his work. Clearly that was behind his madness. He conceived of the Russian Revolution as a need for power and change. That montage at the end of the first act sums up his political beliefs. One's sexual potency, one's drive into life, and that was all in that footage."

The next step was assembling a cast and crew.

For the part of Louise Bryant, the writer who becomes John Reed's wife, Warren cast Diane Keaton, mainly on the basis of her dramatic work in *Looking for Mr. Goodbar*; he told *Goodbar*'s director, Richard Brooks, that he'd been overwhelmed by Diane's performance.

As Eugene O'Neill, the brilliant playwright with whom Bryant has an affair, Beatty cast his friend Jack Nicholson; in real life, of course, the two had had Michelle Phillips in common.

For the role of Whigham, the wealthy publisher, Beatty chose another old friend, George Plimpton. He offered Plimpton the role during a party at Hugh Hefner's house, causing writer Aaron Latham, in an article in *Rolling Stone*, to quip, "And now Warren Beatty, the Playboy of the Movies, was . . . in the Playboy Mansion casting his movie about the Playboy of the Revolution."

Yet another friend, novelist Jerzy Kosinski, was tapped for the part of the Bolshevik bureaucrat Grigory Zinoviev, while Maureen Stapleton was signed on as the feminist organizer Emma Goldman.

Beatty cast his actors in his own inimitable way. For example, he invited Edward Herrmann to his house on Mulholland Drive, then escorted him into an office where one of the first things the actor noticed was a photograph of his wife, Leigh Curran, on the bulletin board. "Do you know her?" Beatty asked innocently, seeing the wide-eyed expression on Herrmann's face.

When Herrmann answered in the affirmative, he asked, "Do you work well with her?"

After Herrmann revealed that the actress in the photo was his wife, Beatty laughed. "Yeah, I know she's your wife," he said. "But do you work well together?"

The result of the meeting was that Herrmann got the part of Eastman and Curran played Eastman's wife. Though the two had never worked together previously, Herrmann assured Beatty he thought they would have no problems.

Next Beatty started lining up his crew. He had already been working with Vittorio Storaro (cameraman on *Apocalypse Now* and Bertolucci's *1900*) on the witness interviews. Now he added Richard Sylbert as set designer and Shirley Russell (director Ken's wife) as costume designer; he also contracted with Stephen Sondheim to do the soundtrack. For this production, he wanted only the best.

Just as he had encouraged Arthur Penn to take his time (and as many takes as needed) when he was directing *Bonnie and Clyde,* so he now encouraged Sylbert to take as much preparation as was necessary in choosing the locations and designing the sets. This was important for two reasons: first, two-thirds of *Reds* required sets, so it was imperative that they be perfect; second, since the action takes place in the years surrounding the Russian Revolution, all actual locations had to fit the time period, with no embarrassing anachronisms.

Because *Reds* takes place in so many settings, Sylbert had his hands full finding suitable locations. Two years before the scene was finally shot, Sylbert had settled upon shooting the Flatiron Building in Manhattan from a certain angle, slanting it so that a carefully positioned double-decker bus would block out the surrounding skyscrapers, bringing the Flatiron into perspective as the skyscraper of 1916.

Many of the exterior scenes could not be shot where they had originally taken place. A diligent search led Sylbert to the house in Croton-on-Hudson, New York, that Reed and Bryant had occupied during the early days of their marriage. When it turned out that the crew couldn't shoot there, Sylbert copied the interiors and reconstructed them on sets in London. For the exterior of the house, he found an abandoned wooden shell in the English countryside.

Provincetown, Massachusetts, was relocated in Twickenham, a quaint village in the London suburbs; the Provincetown beach scenes were shot on the English shore at Camber Sands.

When it came time to search for locations within Russia itself, Beatty, in March of 1979, made the trip with Keaton, Sylbert, and cinematographer Storaro. Beatty, the veteran of several trips to the

country, was, as Sylbert said, "very Russia-wise about the bureaucracy." One of his favorite toasts during the ten days the quartet
spent in the Soviet Union was, "Let us drink to the end of
bureaucracy."

Beatty did not attempt to hide those sentiments from the Russians, either. When he tried to take his friends to Leningrad's revolutionary museum, he was informed by their guide that the
museum was closed. The next day they returned, only to be told
that the museum was closed. Telling the guide he wanted to stretch
his legs a bit, Beatty was soon out of the car and leading the rest of
his party straight to the museum's open front door and into the
museum itself. Not content with having gotten away with this ploy,
Beatty then inquired why the museum contained no pictures of
Trotsky.

Not surprisingly, the Russians informed Beatty that he would
be allowed to shoot inside their country only if he supplied the
government with a script.

The producer (who refused to show a final script even to many
of the actors in the film) refused. In turn, the Russians refused to
allow him to film *Reds* in Russia.

Beatty wasn't about to let the bureaucracy upset his plans. Besides, he—and Sylbert—had already managed to see enough of the
real Russia to create an ersatz one. They decided to shoot in Finland. The capital of that country, Helsinki, contained large areas
built by the same architect who had designed St. Petersburg—
which had become Petrograd during the revolution and is now
Leningrad. Spain would be substituted for the Baku area of southern
Russia.

Beatty's production deal was with Paramount, allegedly the
toughest that studio had ever accepted. Barry Diller, chairman of
Paramount, was the prime negotiator of the deal. But in these days
of megaconglomerates, he was not the most important money man
behind the film. Since Paramount was owned by Gulf and Western
and controlled by G&W chairman, the late Charles Bluhdorn, it
was he who had to be kept happy. As Jerzy Kosinski later remarked,

"John Reed talking to Zinoviev is no different than Warren Beatty talking to Charlie Bluhdorn."

And so *The John Reed Story* metamorphosed into *Comrades* and at last became *Reds*, and the recreation of the Bolshevik Revolution was financed by the epitome of American capitalism, the conglomerate.

As Diller pointed out, "I am sorry to be the one to have to say it, but not one media person, no liberal writer, has pointed out that this big American corporation supported a film that deals with a story that had been buried, a story never told, the absolutely hidden story of the IWW, the American Socialist Party, the American Communist Party. Not one has said, Gulf and Western may be rat bastards but at least they did that."

Diller's remarks must be taken with a healthy grain of salt. The story told in *Reds* had never been buried or suppressed; it was more a case that no one before Beatty had decided it had sufficient entertainment value to be brought to the screen. Paramount's interest in the production was in no way generated by socialistic fervor; on the contrary, Bluhdorn was an immigrant and a fiercely patriotic capitalist whose interest in *Reds* focused on the green it would bring in.

It is to Beatty's credit that he managed to make the story of Reed's revolutionary zeal acceptable to both the money men and the general public, just as it is admirable that he managed to cram so much political material into a film that had to be a love story to succeed commercially.

Successfully bringing *Reds* to the screen in any way, shape, or form was enough in itself to foster Beatty's identification with the subject of the movie. As Jerzy Kosinski put it, "Warren's predicament was: how do I sell to the American people the idea of John Reed? Just as John Reed's predicament was: how do I convey to the American people the idea of the revolution? What faced Warren was the same thing that faced John Reed. He could have been killed by the company town, could have died an artistic death, and been buried in the wall of Hollywood. Just as John Reed reclaimed for America a part of the future, Warren reclaimed for this country a part of its past. Beatty was writing his own *Ten Days That Shook the World*—only his is three hours long, with an intermission."

Beatty accomplished his goal by concentrating as faithfully as possible on the romance between Reed and Louise Bryant and it is to his credit, once again, that the political ramifications don't get swamped by the sometimes corny and melodramatic love story.

To blend these elements into a homogenous, effective whole, Beatty took some license with the facts, shrewdly choosing, as reviewer Kenneth Turan writing in *California Magazine* pointed out, "Hollywood over history." For instance, Louise Bryant did not search for Reed in Finland before surprising him by showing up at a Russian railroad station; she knew he was no longer in Finland and Reed knew when she was to arrive in Russia. There are other aesthetic changes that differ from the actual events, but these were all undertaken to enhance the drama, and, as Turan agreed, "Even Reed—a great populizer who once told a friend that what he was after in his own writing was overall impression, not photographic accuracy—would probably approve."

But approval, disapproval, or any reviews at all were a long way in the future when *Reds* started shooting on August 6, 1979. It would be two and a half years before the movie was released, and Beatty would have 750,000 feet of film, running for a grand total of 130 hours and having devoured a budget estimated at anything between $33.5 and $50 million, before he had finished shooting and was ready to edit what would emerge as *Reds*.

16

MASTERPIECE OR MONSTER?

The making of *Reds* is as epic a tale of filmmaking as *Ten Days That Shook the World* was an epic saga of revolution.

Shooting the film required ten months and the transporting of cast, crew, and equipment from America to England, Spain, and Finland. Deducting time for travel to and from the various locations, there were some 240 days of solid shooting at an estimated $50,000 daily cost, *excluding* script costs, salaries for the film's stars, and Beatty's own fee as director and producer. It's not surprising that, as the shooting went on and on and on, Hollywood wags started predicting that the actual Bolshevik Revolution was going to look like a bargain by the time the final figures were in for *Reds*.

There was a lot of trouble along the way. "Trouble," as Richard Sylbert said, "you either deal with or you might as well forget the whole thing."

Some of the trouble was with Paramount itself, which was not at all happy with the megaproduction it had ended up financing. As Barry Diller later explained to Aaron Latham, "Producing *Reds* was misunderstood by all of us. It was miscalculated. What happened was no preproduction work was done on the film; we had to start immediately because of the availability of the actors. So it was always catch-up. It was originally budgeted at $20 million. It should have been budgeted in the high twenties or low thirties. I got very frustrated, because the film was clearly going to cost vastly more than contemplated. My knee-jerk reaction was to get angry with Warren. And at the worst stage, I just refused to talk to him. I thought that would have some effect. That was naive. Hurtful. Cruel. My behavior was unfortunate."

Diller refused to accept Beatty's phone calls for six weeks before flying to London on Thanksgiving, 1979, to get his relationship with *Reds'* producer back on an even keel. When he returned to London again, just before Christmas, Beatty had five hours of film waiting for him. Pleased with what he saw, Diller was now on Beatty's side, and though they continued to fight over the production, from then on, according to Diller, "We fought in our normal territory. You can't work in that process unless you fight. If you have a point, the only way to make it is with a certain level of viciousness or the other person doesn't know you mean it. You have to show you care."

Diller was now ready, not only to show he cared, but to support Beatty one hundred percent. In January of 1980, Paramount president Michael Eisner issued the statement "I certainly don't consider it a project that's out of control" in response to widely publicized rumors that the studio was having what amounted to a collective coronary over the rising production costs. Eisner defined an out-of-control production as "one of those pictures that go two hundred to four hundred percent over budget today, and *Reds* is nothing like that. It isn't a situation like *The Blues Brothers* or *1941*. Warren is a responsible filmmaker who's going over schedule with responsibility, and going over budget by about fifteen to twenty percent."

Translated into dollars, those figures meant millions, but now, with Diller firmly on his side once again, Warren wasn't going to be hassled by the studio (for whom his *Heaven Can Wait* was one of their biggest moneymakers ever).

Other problems with the production continued to blossom, however, and Paramount's hopes to have the picture ready for release by Christmas of 1980 were in vain. There were labor problems, script problems, even a production shutdown while Warren came up with an ending for the film. Elaine May was commuting between New York and Europe; stars were being shutttled about for scenes; in the middle of the filming, Beatty and Diane Keaton flew off to vacation in Barbados.

The trade papers back in America were meanwhile reporting the dire rumors with relish. "It's hoped Warren Beatty doesn't wind up in the red with his *Reds* movie," was the opener for one of Hank Grant's "Rambling Reporter" columns in *The Hollywood Reporter*, while Jack Martin wrote in *The New York Post* that the film had gone $30 million over budget. Even *Variety* seemed to be smacking its lips when it ran a bold-face headline announcing: BEATTY'S 'REDS' MAY SOAR TO $30-MIL AS SECRETS LEAK OUT.

"Secrets" they were, since Beatty's cousin David McLeod, nominally hired as unit publicist, seemed to function as a shield to keep the media out rather than as an information conduit. Still, there was nothing McLeod could do to stop the whispers.

The article, in the March 26, 1980 issue of *Variety*, listed a multitude of items that were raising the cost, including rewrites, overtime, and actors being flown from the States to deliver a mere two or three lines. In addition, it reported, the director had a shooting ratio that was running as high as thirty-five to one (with thirty-four takes left on the cutting room floor) and he sent the film unit first class by train to a site just sixty miles from London, while he and Jack Nicholson flew down by helicopter.

An added expense was the cost of a full British camera crew, which sat about idly while Storaro shot with his own Italian crew members. This was at the insistence of the British union, as was Beatty's agreement to pay all British-based actors used in the film Screen Actors Guild rates (higher than British Actors' Equity rates) as well as stateside television residuals.

Through it all, Beatty was a demon. "Warren was like a field marshal," according to Dick Sylbert. "Every movie is like a war. A little war. A big war."

For *Reds*, it was an expensive war, with Beatty demanding take after take as the production costs rose higher and higher. The cost wasn't all that was rising, either. The actors grew impatient and irritable as their "field marshal" put them through their paces interminably. "Warren was very fastidious," remarked George Plimpton in a great understatement. "He did thirty or forty takes all the time.

Diane almost got broken. I thought he was trying to break her into what Louise Bryant had been like with Reed."

But Keaton wasn't the only cast member forced to repeat a scene up to forty times until the director was satisfied. And even the most seasoned professionals couldn't help but grow testy when Warren told them, "Do it again."

"What do you want me to do?" Maureen Stapleton, playing Emma Goldman, snapped in answer to one of these commands for repetition. "Take off my clothes?"

But Beatty remained unflustered. "I don't know," he admitted. But he added, "Do it again."

Another time, Stapleton as Goldman addressed a crowd of extras playing workers. It was nighttime, and there was a cold rain falling. Without complaint, she did the scene again and again—and yet again. Finally, after an especially good take, the director seemed satisfied. "Great," he said. And then he added, "One more time."

It was too much for Stapleton, who shouted, "Are you out of your fucking mind?" to the applause of the assembled extras. She might have been shouting at a brick wall. Beatty made her do it again.

If Beatty was infuriating, he was also impressive. He knew what he was doing, and in spite of their frustrations, the cast and crew respected him. "He's got an amazing brain, but he doesn't show off," explained Sylbert. "He never says, 'Look at me directing.' He doesn't do phony stuff. He does story. He is never off on story. And while it was a big picture, a lot of the time it was really intimate and we were making it with only four or five people. And you know, all the time we were learning. You couldn't figure out how to do this picture unless you just started doing it."

Some of the cast couldn't figure out what they were doing *while* they were doing it. It was reported that even assistant directors were without copies of the script, and unsuspecting actors were often asked to improvise their dialogue. "Warren Beatty," said actor Edward Herrmann after it was over, "is *mysterium tremendum*. We never saw a script. It was like shooting *Casablanca*."

The three scripts on *Reds* belonged to Beatty, Keaton, and Nicholson. Other actors were given their lines the night before or on the day of the shooting. When Herrmann complained to Keaton about the difficulties of acting without benefit of a script, she assured him, "It doesn't matter. It's all in Warren's head anyway. He keeps changing it all the time."

As the shooting progressed, Beatty identified more and more with the character he was playing. "The more Warren got into the project, the more he saw himself as John Reed," related Kosinski, who was astonished by the change in his friend. "It's the same path. I was with him the last three months. He dressed like John Reed onstage and off. He was in worse shape than Reed. Exhausted. Coughing all the time. Sick. Emaciated. I was so astonished by all this."

One incident caused by Beatty's identification with Reed reads like a farce. Before shooting a scene, Beatty always explained the action and the context in which it took place for the benefit of the extras. In Seville, which was serving as Baku, Beatty spoke fervently for a full hour, explaining what had led Reed to speak in Baku just before his death, making a big point of Reed's belief that the working man was being exploited by the capitalists in America and his corresponding belief that they should rise up. As he spoke, an interpreter repeated, in Spanish, his speech on the rights of the working man.

At the end of his speech, delivered in 105-degree heat, Beatty called for a lunch break. He was then approached by spokesmen for the extras, who had taken his speech very much to heart. Refusing to be exploited by American capitalists, they had formed a union during their lunch hour and now demanded higher wages. Beatty took it all with good sportsmanship, and at the end of negotiations, the extras' pay was raised by about twenty dollars a day.

As Aaron Latham commented, tongue firmly wedged in cheek, "Actually, Warren Beatty was a better John Reed than Reed was, for the workers lost most of the strikes in which Reed got involved; Beatty had led a successful strike—against himself."

Twice in *Reds*, Reed attacks other people for changing his

work, and Beatty went to enormous lengths to make sure all control of his own Reed project remained in his hands. While filming a courtyard scene in Seville in blazing heat, Warren stopped Storaro and his camera crew from moving their equipment onto a podium to begin shooting, suddenly worried that the cameras might prove too heavy for it. While impatient extras stood around in the heat waiting, Warren sent someone to fetch the man who had constructed the podium, who finally arrived and agreed that it needed strengthening. "You have to worry about such details yourself?" a flabbergasted Jerzy Kosinski asked Beatty.

"Do you let anyone else check your manuscript?" he asked the novelist.

In Spain, Beatty's identification with his hero reached its peak. As Reed in Baku had turned down the government's offer of an apartment, moving instead into a cold water shack, Beatty, too, found a shack to live in while he was shooting the Baku scenes. He shared a three-room, cold water house—boasting only a hotplate for cooking and a bathroom door that couldn't be closed—with Kosinski and Kiki von Frauenhofer, the writer's girlfriend.

"Warren was living in this house with me, and I am really Zinoviev," recalled the Polish-born Kosinski, a refugee during the World War II. "For me, as a novelist, I am living in a revolution. But I am also living with this pathetic American. I'm back into my past, like Zinoviev—hot days, cold nights. I'm enjoying it. But I'm living with John Reed, who is doing this ridiculous thing, and I'm annoyed by it. I'm very cynical. To me, it's all a game. To him, it's an idea. And I laugh at him daily. I became just as impatient as Zinoviev. Why was Beatty there? What helped me to become Zinoviev was questioning why this crazy American was doing this crazy thing. I honestly didn't think this was going to work. I thought he was going to be buried in the Kremlin wall again. The analogy would run its course."

Like John Reed, Beatty appeared to thrive on exhaustion, over-work, ill health. Nothing could pressure him into stopping the cameras before that one last take; nothing could dampen the religious fervor with which he approached each new day of shooting. "If Warren has any weakness," his friend and fellow producer Robert Evans once commented, "it's that he spreads himself too thin." With *Reds*, it was inconceivable that one man could shoulder the responsibility for so much—no detail was too small to deserve his personal attention.

At long last, on December 31, 1980, Army Archerd opened his "Just for Variety" column,

Happy New Year: And it must be a happy day at Paramount, now that Warren Beatty has wound up photography on *Reds*. He shot final scenes in D.C. over the weekend and in N.Y. Monday. . . .

Paramount had no cause for immediate celebration. One hundred and thirty hours of film still had to be edited down to a viable length, a gargantuan chore that would add more time and money to the balance sheet. A soundtrack had to be laid down, prints had to be made and color corrected, a trailer had to be created, and, equally important, and ad campaign had to be devised to sell *Reds* to the American public.

And while all this was going on, Beatty knew everyone was wondering if he had another *Heaven's Gate* on his hands, if—like Michael Cimino—he had been given carte blanche only to create a monster unredeemable through editing.

By producing, co-writing, directing, and starring in *Reds*, not to mention owning a piece of the picture, Beatty had surpassed even Orson Welles. Welles dominated the making of *Citizen Kane*, but he owned none of it—and the budget of that classic was under $750,000, the cost of less than four minutes of *Reds* when it was finally cut down to viewing size.

Beatty was well aware there were those who longed to see him fail, if only because he had dared to demand absolute power. And he knew he was going to have to sell *Reds* all the way down the line: to Charles Bluhdorn, to Barry Diller, to the exhibitors, to the moviegoers. But that lay in the future. Before he could even think or worry about how the finished product would fare, he had to take 750,000 feet of rough footage, leave most of it on the cutting room floor, and come up with a movie.

17

RELEASING *REDS*

Early in January, 1981, Warren began editing *Reds*, setting up shop at JRS Productions on West 54th Street in New York. The perfectionist producer assembled a corps of experts to cut and trim the movie into marketable shape. This group was headed by the renowned Dede Allen, who had edited Beatty's *Bonnie and Clyde* as well as Sidney Lumet's *Dog Day Afternoon*, and is considered one of the top pros in the business, and Craig McKay, editor of that wonderful documentary-style movie, Jonathan Demme's *Melvin and Howard* (the subject of which was Beatty's other obsession, Howard Hughes).

One might imagine that after the grueling shooting schedule he had just completed Beatty would have collapsed, or at least taken off and let his editors do the preliminary work without him. But this is the man Buck Henry described as thriving upon work done under pressure, barely sleeping, and doing as much himself as possible.

He ran true to form during the editing process of *Reds*. He was constantly present, watching what Allen, McKay, and their sub-editors were doing. Often, he slept in the cutting room, greeting his editors in the morning with some ideas he had worked on during the night.

Computerization has simplified the editing process, with camera footage transferred to videotape, allowing a range of different splicings to be viewed in minutes. After a decision on editing various pieces of film has been reached from interchanging on video, the final cuts are made on the film itself. Even with the help rendered by the new technology, six months were required to cut the 130 hours of film down to 199 minutes, a final cut/shoot ratio of about forty to one.

Beatty was in remarkable control throughout the entire editing process, and unlike Michael Cimino, he didn't try to hang on to as much footage as possible. Nor, as was the case with Francis Ford Coppola and *Apocalypse Now*, had he shot so many different versions of incidents that it was confusing to decide which to combine to form a cohesive whole. Beatty, nicknamed "the Pro" by his friend Jack Nicholson, showed that he was truly a professional. The longest version of *Reds* after editing ran for 220 minutes; less than half an hour would have to be trimmed for the final version.

During all this post-shooting production work, *Reds* was not available for viewing by anyone not part of the editing team. The aura of secrecy surrounding the movie was as pervasive as it had been while the cameras rolled in Europe.

By September of 1981, Beatty had a four-and-a-half-minute trailer ready to show in theaters; by the beginning of November, the ad campaign was set and the poster ready.

Then, in a screening room on the thirtieth floor of the Gulf and Western building in New York, a special screening was held, at which only three prople were present: Beatty, Barry Diller, and Charles Bluhdorn. Beatty and Diller anxiously awaited Bluhdorn's reaction, and the atmosphere in the posh room was tense.

"It was a very emotional screening," Diller said afterward. "We could have brought shame and degradation on the company. We badly, emotionally, wanted him to say he approved."

To the vast relief of Beatty and Paramount's chairman of the board, the chairman of the board of Gulf and Western loved the film. As the three lingered in the screening room, dining there and talking until one in the morning, Bluhdorn gave *Reds* his seal of approval.

On November 9, the movie was screened for the other top men at Paramount, who emerged from the viewing impressed but worried. Could *Reds* make it in the heartland of America? They had their doubts.

The film was next shown to exhibitors, where it faced another problem. There has long been a campaign in the United States to outlaw the practice of "blind bidding," which has proved financially damaging to theater owners. Under blind bidding, theaters contract to show a film without having had a chance to view it first. The practice is now outlawed in twenty-two states, and it was to exhibitors from those states that *Reds* was shown. The terms were steep—exhibitors were forced to concede a great deal to Paramount in return for the chance to show the film—and many of those who agreed to take the movie on at a risk to themselves did so only after the personal intervention of its producer, who, as always, was committed to selling his film all the way down the line.

Beatty also nipped another obstacle in the bud when the motion picture received an "R" rating. In an emotional appeal, Beatty argued that his film dealt with a forgotten era of American history that should be available for every school-aged child in the country to see, regardless of the adult language of the film. The rating was changed by the appeals hearing to "PG," and the exhibitors were now proud to be part of such a momentous event.

But if Beatty wooed the exhibitors, he remained standoffish toward others, including Paramount's own publicity department, which was barred from daily screenings for the producer's friends and hand-picked critics.

Ten days before the scheduled December 4 countrywide opening of the film, Beatty was still virtually holed up in an apartment down the block from the JRS offices, selecting stills, recutting trailers, fighting with the labs over the color corrections, and revising advertising copy.

Beatty refused to talk to the press, unquestionably feeding their thirst for his downfall and stirring up the rumors that *Reds* was destined to be a bomb because of its length and the unpalatable subject matter. With a pre-Christmas opening, there was an extra factor involved. Not only is the Christmas rush to the theaters traditionally followed by an enormous lull, but holiday audiences tend to prefer lighter fare, the hit of the year before having been *Stir Crazy*.

Through it all, the producer had no comment, remaining equally silent on Arthur Knight's pre-release rave review and Robert Osborne's negative review when they appeared together in *The Hollywood Reporter*.

There was, however, one review Beatty actively sought. The political liberal set up a private screening at the White House for the conservative president in search of kind words from Reagan for his movie about a Communist radical.

As Kosinki compared Beatty and Reed: "When John Reed finished *Ten Days That Shook the World*, he took his book to Lenin and said, 'Please give me a good quote.' And one of the first people Warren showed his *Ten Days* to was Reagan. And he asked for a quote. Lenin gave a quote. And Reagan gave a quote."

The president's quote was to the effect that he liked the movie, though he wished there had been a happy ending. Beatty now had two important approvals under his belt—those of the head of Gulf and Western and the chief of state.

And so, on December 4, 1981, *Reds* opened simultaneously in almost 300 movie theaters across America, a three-hour-and-nineteen-minute epic that could be screened only twice a night because of its monumental length.

The reviews were mixed, though few critics were unimpressed with Beatty's accomplishment. While not everyone agreed with David Israel's contention that *Reds* was "a picture that works on every level," it was well-nigh impossible to dispute his claim that ". . . Warren Beatty has made his lasting mark on film, has provided the innovation, has become the man who created the movie as journalism and journalism as the movie."

What makes *Reds* work is that it is, first and foremost, a romance and not a political tract. Beatty deserves the title "the Pro" because when it comes to comprehending the requirements of commercialism, he is professional enough to realize that audiences want love and not rhetoric, and that they even prefer their romances a bit on the soupy side. (Hence the "cutesy" scenes of the dog scratching at the door again and again while Reed and Bryant make love, Reed burning dinner, and Diane Keaton racing red-nosed across the steppes in search of the man she loves.)

The fact is, even for those who adored and were influenced by the movie, politics were soft-pedaled in *Reds*; they presented no threat. As Kenneth Turan, one of those who liked the film, wrote, "*Reds* is no threat to the Republic; the revolution will not be coming courtesy of Paramount Pictures. While interested parties have been huffing and puffing about what a brave and daring thing it is to make a major motion picture about the lives of American radicals John Reed and Louise Bryant, Warren Beatty—producer, director, co-writer, star, and all-around sly dog—has done what nobody expected but everyone should have. He's gone and made a *movie*, a very long and satisfying romance wherein Reed's devotion to godless communism provides the most exotic of backgrounds for an old-fashioned love story that few moviegoers will have any difficulty recognizing or embracing."

Not everyone was captivated by the film; some reviews found *Reds* boring, overlong, and, in general, too much ado about not much of anything. Some, like Rex Reed, asserted it wasn't that John Reed's politics were antagonistic that made the movie hard to take so much as the fact that John Reed himself wasn't an especially interesting or admirable subject for a film in the first place.

"The point is," Reed wrote in his review of *Reds* for the New York *Daily News* on December 7, 1981, "that a man is a hero as long as he dies for what he believes, even if nobody else does. But why should we remember him? He changed nothing, made no impact, and influenced no succeeding generations. If truth was told, he was probably something of a nut. I respect Warren Beatty for following his dreams, but what good does it do if you end up talking to yourself?"

Little fault was found with the direction or the acting. Beatty, whose physical resemblance to Reed was notable, directed himself in a capable and very human performance, stressing Reed's idealism and vulnerability in a manner calculated to make him a sympathetic hero rather than a radical nut case; Diane Keaton, in a difficult role (according to *Reds*, Louise Bryant spent most of her time trailing after Reed and whining), managed to convey her character's pain and frustration at loving a man who loved causes more than people; Maureen Stapleton, who had balked at shooting a scene yet another time, received an Academy Award for her striking performance; Kosinski was applauded for his transition from writer to actor; Jack Nicholson turned in one of his best performances as world-weary, contemptuous Eugene O'Neill, who seduces Bryant but can't hope to win her away from Reed.

The movie was released in time to be eligible for 1981 Academy Award consideration, and everyone waited anxiously to see if *Reds* would edge out *On Golden Pond* (the other top contender) for Best Picture of 1981. *Reds* had already amassed the most nominations with twelve to *Golden Pond*'s ten, also setting a record for the most nominations for any single film since 1966. Now the world was waiting to see if *Reds* would get official confirmation as Warren Beatty's masterpiece.

Some, like Jack Nicholson, felt the time had come for Beatty to receive accolades. "In the past," he said, "the Academy has always been a little hesitant to give the Pro his due. They hold back because he's so pretty and cute."

In the meantime, during the period between *Reds'* release and the Oscar ceremonies, rumors flew that regardless of how much critical recognition the film might be garnering, it was not a commercial success. The blame for this was laid squarely at its producer's feet.

Rona Barrett, during her spot on the "Today" show, was the first to accuse Beatty of sabotaging his own creation. Referring to him as a man "who is often credited with playing the media the way Isaac Stern plays the violin," she pointed out that Beatty was doing nothing to personally promote the film. He sold it to the exhibitors, but he was unwilling to exert himself to sell *Reds* to the press and the public.

Then, in April of '82, the New York *Daily News* carried a report that *Reds* was "doing dismally," drawing an average of only fifty-seven people per performance at ten Manhattan theaters. The report carried a quote from an unidentified "marketing insider" who accused Beatty of having only himself to blame for making the movie a loser, saying, "He may have committed the biggest faux pas in the last fifty years of filmmaking by opting to play the prima donna, making himself unavailable for publicity." And, according to another *Daily News* source, Beatty's charisma, had he chosen to promote his production, could have pulled in revenues as high as $25 million.

Why did Beatty—who took such an active role in promoting the other films he produced—decide not to publicize *Reds* personally? Thus far, he has not answered that question, and it isn't easy to come up with a reason. Perhaps the strain of making the film had finally overtaken him and he didn't have an extra reservoir of strength to deal with the media. Perhaps he was determined to let this motion picture, so dear to his heart, stand on its own two feet. Or perhaps he just couldn't be bothered. With Warren Beatty, it's almost always a mystery. As Robert Benton, co-writer of *Bonnie and Clyde*, said shortly after *Reds'* release, "There is an aspect of Warren in Clyde Barrow. There is a part of him that is an outlaw. He's chosen to be aloof. I think he's always remained outside the movie business. He's never won an Academy Award."

Now, Warren again chose to remain aloof, while his friends worried that his lack of cooperation with the press would keep *Reds* in the red and continue to keep that gold statuette out of Beatty's hands. But Warren's obsession of more than a decade had burned itself out in expression. Now he hungered for a new venture, new stimulation. *Reds* was relegated to the past, and, along with it, his romance with Diane Keaton. That relationship had been consumed by the obsession that had drawn Warren to her in the first place: the need for someone who could be his Louise Bryant both on and off the screen.

18

BEATTY'S OWN BRYANT

In discussing his friend Warren Beatty's rsemblance to John Reed, Jack Nicholson said, "*Reds* is about the conflict between the private man and the socially active man. It is about giving up your private life to a tremendous degree."

He then referred to John Reed's attempt to meld his public life with his private life by involving the women in that life with his work. "Just look at how many movies the Pro's made with his girlfriends," he pointed out. "Of course, there are classic pitfalls. Making a movie is psychologically brutal."

Warren's relationship with Diane Keaton fell victim to those pitfalls. Lovers before *Reds* began shooting, they were no longer a steady twosome by the time of its release.

Like Beatty, Diane Keaton is an enigma. An Oscar winner, a talented singer, a skilled photographer, she still resembles a little girl dressing up and afraid of being caught at it. Unlike the other women with whom Warren has been smitten, Keaton does not radiate self-confidence.

Born Diane Hall in Los Angeles on January 5, 1946, Diane is the eldest of four children born to Jack and Dorothy Hall. Though Mr. and Mrs. Hall are now divorced, they were very much married when Diane was growing up; her upbringing in Los Angeles and Santa Ana, California was as all-American as the proverbial apple pie. Her father was well-to-do, an engineer and then a real estate broker; her mother, a semiprofessional photographer, was once the winner of the Mrs. Los Angeles contest.

As little Henry Warren Beatty used to do show business imitations, so did young Diane Hall sing along to Judy Garland and Doris Day records. She wanted to be a singer when she grew up, and it was as a singer that she made her stage debut. A ninth-grader, she blacked out her front teeth and sang "All I Want for Christmas Is My Two Front Teeth" with a classmate.

She capitulated immediately to the magic of the spotlight, and by her senior year in high school, she was one of her school's established actresses, with a leading role in their production of *Little Mary Sunshine*.

Like Warren, Diane decided college was not for her. After one semester at Santa Ana College and a few months at Orange Coast College, she'd had enough. A drama coach suggested she study her craft at Sanford Meisner's prestigious Neighborhood Playhouse in New York City, so the entire Hall family packed up and traveled along with her to check it out. In 1965, she began studying at the school on a scholarship.

Diane, who had started using Keaton, her mother's maiden name, for professional purposes, finished at the Neighborhood Playhouse and, following in the footsteps of Beatty, did her share of summer stock. Like Warren's, her first big break came via Broadway, when she was cast in the rock musical *Hair*, where she distinguished herself by refusing to strip with the rest of the cast for the show's big shocker (which, after shows like *O, Calcutta!* seems tame indeed).

Her next big break—and a long-lasting relationship—came when she was cast by Woody Allen to play the lead opposite him in *Play It Again, Sam*, his first Broadway show and a milestone in that it took him from stand-up comedy into a new career.

Had Diane been any taller, her autobiography would be a different story. At five foot seven, she topped Allen by a mere three-quarters of an inch, a size discrepancy he decided he could live with.

Live with it he did. The two set up housekeeping during the run of *Play It Again, Sam*, and for several years, Woody was not only her man, he was also her favorite director. He remained the latter after their offscreen affair ended (of all Woody's films she has been in, only *Play It Again, Sam, Sleeper,* and *Love and Death* were made before their breakup).

Obviously, the two have remained close since they stopped living together, and are each other's biggest boosters. When he wrote *Annie Hall* for her, Woody not only gave Diane her chance to walk off with the Academy Award, he gave her the most loving Valentine any man could give to his former lover. Still, in spite of the effect he has had on her life and career, both Diane and Woody insist she would have made it without his help.

"I've made contributions to her life, but not nearly as profound contributions as she's made to mine," Woody has confessed. "I never had a good understanding of people; she has an uncanny understanding of people—when they are vulnerable, when they are covering up, when they are hostile."

Annie Hall captures the essence of Diane and Woody's own love story. Though the facts aren't the same, they both admit the characters are true to themselves. The way in which Diane explained *Annie Hall*'s popularity can be said to describe not only her relationship with Allen, but also her relationship with Warren Beatty, now in the past.

"First," she said, "it affects couples so much because everybody knows, I think, how difficult it is to have a relationship and to keep it alive and continuing. So there's a universal fact of life that says breaking up happens to everybody, so no one should feel like a failure when it does happen.

"Then, it's also sort of Pygmalion, you know. He teaches her and guides her, but then she goes off on her own when she finds the relationship becoming too insular, too confining, too negative, and so she proceeds out into her own life. But in the end, they're still friends, they still like each other, and they know they can't go back to the way it once was. That's touching, you know, it's sort of bittersweet, the idea that you still have a lot of affection for this person but you both know that too much time and change has taken place. But life is time and change, and it just cannot always be worked out, no matter how much affection there may be. I personally feel that I want to have my own life and work and be with somebody who thinks of me as an equal, you know, and that's what's important for everybody."

Warren Beatty discovered Diane before he signed her to co-star in *Reds*; they were a firmly entrenched couple by the time shooting began. Beatty is, as ever, reluctant to discuss a woman with whom he has been involved, but what he does say about Diane reveals that he was attracted to the same qualities in her that Woody found so irresistible.

"She's constantly in search of something that's true," the man who puts so much emphasis on candor says admiringly. "She has no interest in the delivery of a punch line; she cares only about the true situation, which then gives a wonderful dignity to a great joke writer like Woody. And in a film with political implications, she searches for what's true in a person and absolves the situation of being preachy or propagandistic. In other words, she has a built-in bullshit detector."

An almost idealistic respect for honesty turned out to be only one of the many things these two seemingly antithetical people shared. Both are far from glib offscreen, punctuating their conversation with plenty of "ums," "ahs," and, in Keaton's case, "you knows." Both have a love of music that started in childhood. Both are, by nature, loners who have learned to live with the gregariousness that's a requirement of their trade. And both are private people who refuse to talk about their private lives.

Unlike Beatty, Keaton would never come right out and bluntly state, "My life is not for public consumption. Yes, I owe the public something for the attention they've given me and for the monies I've earned, but not my insides. No one owes anyone that." Instead, she gracefully sidesteps questions that threaten her privacy.

Singer/songwriter Nick Holmes, who appeared with Diane when she sang at Reno Sweeney's in the early seventies and has since worked with her on a possible album which would feature Diane singing her own lyrics, found her friendly but introverted.

During the long breaks between shows, when the two would sit around the dressing rooms backstage at the Greenwich Village nightclub (no longer in existence), Diane preferred playing movie games—her favorite being the one where one person names a movie, the other names an actor in that movie, the first person then names another movie with that actor in it, the other person then names another actor in the new movie, ad infinitum—to conversing on a more personal level.

"I really liked her," he recalled, "and I always felt sure she was doing something to maintain her privacy. She never came off it. I don't think she wanted many people to know her. You know, she'd be coy enough to be unbelievable, but it was always attractive enough that you didn't care if it was an act. And I never thought she herself was that aware that she was doing it. Which made it even more attractive. I'd describe her as just being very private."

She was certainly very private where Warren Beatty was concerned. After *Reds*, Diane went on to co-star with Albert Finney in *Shoot the Moon*, giving a performance many critics thought was her best yet. The film, directed by Alan Parker (*Fame*, *Midnight Express*), dealt with the breakup of a marriage. It was during the filming of *Shoot the Moon* that Beatty and Keaton split up, but Diane didn't reveal any of her feelings to her co-workers. "If anyone mentioned Big W," Parker related, "she'd just walk away. There was no way she was going to share all that."

Warren had no comment on the rupture of their relationship, though he did not amend a former admission that, "Whenever a relationship has ended, the decision has never been mine. It's always been the other person's. And no matter what happened, I've never felt very far apart from any of the women with whom I've been involved. Some feeling always remains."

Keaton is no exception to at least one part of that rule. She and Beatty have remained on excellent terms since calling it quits, and it would surprise no one were the two to rediscover deeper feeling toward each other now that the strain of doing *Reds* together is far in the past.

The girl who said she "never had much success getting dates" in high school and who always seemed amazed that people really liked her took to her romance with the playboy of motion pictures like a duck to water. Rather than seeming stunned that a ladykiller of Beatty's reputation would want her, she was, publicly at least, totally relaxed in the relationship. Nor did she attempt to impress the jet-setter on his own level. Instead, she took him to visit her family and showed him the 8mm home movie pantomine the Halls had made of *Bonnie and Clyde*—with a youthful Diane Hall taking the part of Clyde Barrow. "Warren broke up," according to Jack Hall, Diane's father. "He wanted to see her over and over."

Warren has admitted that in his opinion sex changes a relationship and can be traumatizing because it leaves the partners vulnerable. As someone who finds vulnerability a trauma in itself, he couldn't help but be drawn to a woman whose unabashed vulnerability has always set her apart. "Diane has a great sense of the terror that a woman can feel who has an insecure identity," he once said. "And she has a great sense of the comedic aspects of that terror."

In *Reds*, Louise Bryant's vulnerability and insecurity was no laughing matter—it was the core of Bryant's relationship with Reed, what kept them together and drove them apart. "I'm tired of living in your margins—I'm not taken seriously when you're around," Bryant attacks Reed in the movie. And yet she acknowledges that her need for him has made her "a boring, clinging, miserable" companion.

Did Diane decide during the filming of *Reds* that the open, vulnerable side of her needed more nurturing than Beatty was able to give her? It's no secret that the two fought constantly during the filming, and it would be impossible to keep such tension between the director and the leading lady from spilling over into their private life together.

Aaron Latham, in looking over Jerzy Kosinski's book of personal photographs taken during the shooting of *Reds*, noticed how many of the pictures showed Keaton standing in front of the camera, angrily arguing with the man behind that camera, her scowling director. "These were not moments of absence of tension," Kosinski told him. "It was not easy directing Diane."

Did she expect velvet glove treatment because she was the director's girlfriend? Did Beatty go too far in browbeating her into his image of Louise Bryant? Did the explosive quality of the Reed/Bryant relationship overtake the easygoing camaraderie of the Beatty/Keaton romance until nothing salvageable remained? No one will ever know the answer to those questions for certain, perhaps not even Warren and Diane. The sparks between the two ignited the screen and made *Reds* a great love story. But when the movie was ended, so was the love affair, though it had been on an even keel for the year preceding the actual shooting of the film. And perhaps the last word on the subject will be Jack Nicholson's, who, when asked if John Reed and Louise Bryant would have stayed together if Reed hadn't died in Russia, answered emphatically, "No way!"

By February of 1980, the strain was evident, and Nigel Dempster, London's chief diarist and gossip columnist, was reporting that the romance was on its last legs and that Diane had turned down not one but two proposals of marriage from one of the world's most eligible bachelors.

Before long, Warren was openly escorting other women to dinners and parties, though he continued to see Diane as well, showing up with her to catch *42nd Street* on Broadway between dates with Mary Tyler Moore, Hope Lange, and top model Janice Dickinson.

The transition from exclusivity to a casual relationship appeared to be painless. In 1982, Diane sat by Warren's side at the Academy Awards ceremony, where their mutual affection and ease with one another was evident. Keaton was a leading contender for the Best Actress Oscar, and when co-star Maureen Stapleton was rewarded for her superb supporting performance as Emma Goldman, it appeared that the odds for winning that statuette were with Diane as well. But if she felt any disappointment when the laurels went instead to Katharine Hepburn for *On Golden Pond*, she didn't show it, applauding Miss Hepburn's win with as much enthusiasm as the rest of the audience. Perhaps the widespread prediction at the time that she was certain to garner another nomination the following year for *Shoot the Moon* was consolation enough.

Diane and Warren still refuse to comment on why they drifted apart, letting others draw their conclusions. Keaton, for one, tries not to worry too much about what people may think of her, in relation to Beatty and everything else, because ". . . that can sort of destroy your life, even though it's honorable and you are lucky and all the rest of that. But if you're caught up all the time in what people are thinking of you, how can you have any freedom to take a look outside yourself? It will drive you nuts."

Diane is looking to the future, working on her music as well as her acting, sticking close to her bright, airy apartment high over Central Park on Manhattan's West Side, which she shares with her three cats. The walls are covered with photographs artfully illuminated by track lighting. A talented photographer (much of her own work is featured in *Annie Hall*), she has had a show of her photos as well as a book published. In view of Beatty's propensity for setting up housekeeping in luxury hotels, it's ironic that one of Diane's favorite photographic subjects is the hotel lobby. Her studies of barren, run-down, unpopulated hotel lounges poignantly capture the loneliness of transient living.

Beatty, predictably, is already immersed in the pre-production work involved in bringing his Howard Hughes docudrama to the screen. Like Reed, like Hughes, he is most passionate not about people, but about accomplishment. As he himself admitted all the way back in 1962, "I don't know what I do for fun. I don't say work is one thing and fun is another. I have fun working, I hope, and if I don't have fun working, I'm not happy."

19

THE NEXT OBSESSION

In March of 1982, Beatty was awarded the feature film award by the Directors Guild of America, a major step on the road to the recognition of *Reds* as a great motion picture. It was also a promising omen for the upcoming Oscar ceremonies. Since 1948, the winner of the Directors Guild award has gone on to win the Academy Award as well, with only two exceptions: the Directors Guild winners of 1968 and 1972 were Anthony Harvey and Francis Ford Coppola for, respectively, *Lion in Winter* and *The Godfather*, but directorial Oscars in those two years went to Carol Reed for *Oliver!* and Bob Fosse for *Cabaret*.

The awards banquet was held simultaneously at New York's Plaza Hotel and the Beverly Hilton in Los Angeles. Accepting in Los Angeles, Warren gave a gracious speech in which he thanked almost his entire cast and crew, singling out Diane Keaton as one "whose acting integrity can hold a movie together," and Jack Nicholson, "whose integrity can hold a director together."

Modest as always when it comes to public speaking, Warren told the assembled crowd, "Making a movie is a very hard thing to do. And I'm not sure how anybody ever does it."

He then delivered a special tribute to the executives at Paramount who had stuck by him through the long and costly production period. "Only in America," he said patriotically, "could a film with this subject matter and this size be made without censorship from the people who put up the money."

Beatty's Directors Guild win increased the feeling that, in spite of its poor showing at the box office so far, *Reds* might turn out to be a winner all the way down the line, and by the time Oscar night rolled around, *On Golden Pond* was considered the single contender that might edge out *Reds* when the Best Picture award was announced.

Instead, the dark horse came in first. *Chariots of Fire*, from Britain, was as lush and socially conscious a production as *Reds*, and if an unexpected winner, it was a well-received one (except by those chauvinists who abhorred the idea of a non-American movie edging out the home grown variety).

Beatty's consolation prize, for which he appeared properly moved and gratified, was the Oscar for Best Director, giving him, on his first solo attempt, the two most prestigious prizes a director could receive.

The award was welcomed as enthusiastically by the movie's backers as it was by the film's director, since it would be a draw at the box office. For *Reds*, recognized work of art or not, was doing as badly commercially as its detractors had predicted. With costs of approximately $100 million to make up just to break even, the film had grossed only $35 million in the four months of its release.

For Beatty, though, winning the Oscar was both the culmination and the termination of his personal involvement. Though *Reds'* grosses would directly affect his bankability as a producer, he put the film behind him. He was already immersed in his next project. By July, he was embroiled in meetings with Greg Bautzer, attorney for the Summa Corporation, busily acquiring the Hughes corporation's rights to part of Howard Hughes' life story.

And so Beatty has gone on to his next obsession, one that has existed as long as his fixation on Reed. Just as he related to Reed's conflict between his personal desires and his political beliefs, so he has since his salad days been transfixed by Hughes' uses and abuses of power. "What *interests* me about Howard Hughes?" he blurted to one reporter, stunned that anyone could fail to be entranced by the reclusive billionaire. "It has to do with becoming a victim of your own accumulated power."

Even before Beatty had acquired much power of his own, he was tantalized by the mythic proportions of the former filmmaker, by his wealth and paranoia (and the secrecy that went hand in hand with the latter) and by the power he wielded. According to Leslie Caron, Hughes kept rooms at the Beverly Wilshire at the same time she was sharing Beatty's penthouse suite there, and the actor was relentless in his attempts to discover if the billionaire was in residence. And, while dodging interviews himself, Beatty never gave up trying to get his own interviews with Hughes' bodyguards.

The Hughes project, like *Reds*, has already been years in the making. As long ago as April 1976, Warner Brothers announced that Beatty would be starring in and producing the film version of Howard Hughes' life. At that time, Warren said, "I've been working on the screenplay for a number of months, and the intention is to direct it myself at the moment.

"It's something I've been developing for some time. It seemed now that I should go ahead and do it. It's a character and a phenomenon that I feel rather strongly about."

When someone pointed out to him that in *The Fortune*, with his mustache and slicked-down, parted hair, he resembled the young Howard Hughes, he agreed, "People have said that for years."

Beatty's fascination with Hughes is not unique. Few who followed the life and times of the enigmatic tycoon until his death in the spring of 1976 failed to be titillated by the man who had everything most people ever dreamed of, only to choose the reclusive existence of an eccentric hermit.

The parallels between the lives of Beatty and Hughes don't reach back to their childhoods. Hughes' father, a wealthy man, died when his son was only nineteen, leaving his heir his share in the Hughes Tool Company. Hughes, a mechanical genius, invented the "Spruce Goose," the largest plane ever to fly (at 320 feet long, it is sixty percent longer than a Boeing 747). An economic wheeler and dealer, his holdings at one time or another included Trans World Airlines (he sold his 78 percent share in 1966 for $566 million), RKO Pictures, Nevada hotels and casinos, TV networks, a helicopter company, Hughes Airwest, various mines, an architectural firm, and vast amounts of income property.

A true adventurer, Hughes entered the motion picture business at the age of twenty-one, producing such films as *Hell's Angels*, featuring the young Jean Harlow, *Scarface*, *The Front Page*, and *The Outlaw* (which starred Jane Russell in her Hughes-designed cantilevered brassiere). "Hughes was an excellent editor," said Gordon Youngman, a former RKO executive. "In fact, he was too much of a perfectionist—he took so much time editing that his pictures didn't make money."

If there are intimations of Beatty in Hughes' perfectionism, there are even more in Hughes' taste for beautiful actresses. He dated such goddesses of the silver screen as Ava Gardner, Ida Lupino, Lana Turner, Loretta Young, and Katharine Hepburn before he discovered Jean Peters in 1947. The two married ten years later; coincidentally, 1957 was the last time Hughes allowed himself to be photographed. He and Peters were divorced in 1971.

It was when Hughes was in his fifties that his oddness changed him from eccentric genius to bizarre recluse. His hypochondria reached grotesque proportions: He kept boxes of tissues near him at all times, refusing to touch anyone or anything without first covering his hands with Kleenex; he sat around naked because he believed clothing carried germs; he forbade his aides to eat onions, garlic, or Roquefort dressing on the basis that they were "breath destroyers."

For the last two decades of his life, Hughes lived as a hermit, moving secretly from hotel to hotel until 1966, when he arrived at the service entrance of his Desert Inn Hotel in Las Vegas in a panel truck, stepped into an elevator that conveyed him to the ninth-floor penthouse, and was never seen again except by doctors, aides, bellhops, and immigration officials. In 1972, when he held a telephone press conference to deny the legitimacy of Clifford Irving's fake "biography," Hughes was asked why he lived the way he did. "I don't know," he answered simply. "I sort of slid into it."

Though his old adviser Noah Dietrich insisted Hughes had no politics, he contributed almost religiously to anyone he thought could further his own interests, telling Dietrich, "Everyone has a price." Some of those to whom Hughes contributed are firm Beatty friends like Birch Bayh and Alan Cranston. His donations were bipartisan: Though he gave money to help clear up JFK's campaign costs, and in support of Hubert Humphrey, he also contributed to Richard Nixon's 1962 race for governor of California and made a large loan to Nixon's brother Donald.

When Hughes died at seventy, his six-foot-four-inch frame had shrunk two inches and he weighed only ninety pounds. The man who had done so much for the aircraft industry died in flight, while he was being airlifted from Acapulco (he had surreptitiously set up residence at the Acapulco Princess Hotel in 1975) for emergency medical care in Houston. Perhaps Walter Kane, director of Hughes Hotels, summed up the story of the billionaire's life when he observed, "It is tragic that Howard Hughes had to die to prove he was alive."

"I think it's not impossible," Warren Beatty said confidently when the difficulty of getting reliable information on Hughes was pointed out. "I think it's somebody I know something about."

Though he is nowhere near the late magnate in terms of riches, power, or eccentricity, Beatty can find common ground in most areas. Considering Hughes' life in hotel suites, his inability to find lasting happiness with any one of the beautiful women in his life, and his love of intrigue, fetish for privacy, and mushrooming hypochondria, it's understandable that Beatty might feel an even more all-encompassing identification with Hughes than he did with the man laid to rest within the Kremlin walls. Though Beatty's concern with his own health has never approached that of Hughes, as good a friend as Mike Nichols calls him "a postgraduate hypochondriac."

There is no reason to believe that Beatty will be any less dedicated a producer on his Hughes bio-pic than he's been on his former productions. In this case, his drive for perfection will complement

Hughes' own nitpicking as a filmmaker. Like Hughes, he knows his editing and pays special—and time-consuming—attention to the editing process. But when it comes to bearing the full weight of responsibility for a motion picture, Beatty outdoes even Hughes. After making *Heaven Can Wait*, he defended himself against criticism that he was too obsessed with too many details as a producer. "Anyone who would make films and ignore the final phase—how it's projected on the screen, the speakers in the theater—is not realistic," he reasoned. "You can put in years and have the entire thing erased by a light bulb. As the producer, I have nobody to blame but myself if the movie doesn't come off."

One would think that preparing a production with such single-mindedness would mean giving up everything else, but for Beatty, the early stages of a project still leave him spare time to consider other projects as well. Though in the past few years he has shown no great interest in appearing in any other producer's films, he continues to be offered parts, many of which would be impossible for another actor even to consider refusing.

In addition to the lead in *Charlie Boy*, Beatty is also a favorite for the lead role of the clever, charismatic mass murderer in Mark Rydell's screen adaptation of the late Tommy Thompson's best-selling book, *Serpentine*. He's been offered the lead in another feature film, *Tequila Sunrise*, and is said to be considering co-starring in a remake of *San Francisco* with his buddy Jack Nicholson. Then, too, his old friend and *Shampoo* co-author Robert Towne, who successfully made his own switch to directing with *Personal Best*, has written a new screenplay and would like his former mentor for the star.

Another who's interested in Beatty as an actor is Claus von Bulow, the social lion convicted for the attempted murder of his wealthy wife. If von Bulow has his way, Warren will portray him in a television mini-series based on the tragedy and the notorious trial. Never one for idleness, Beatty also talked with Blake Edwards about starring in the remake of François Truffaut's gently satirical tale of a modern-day womanizer, *The Man Who Loved Women*, to be written and directed by Edwards (Burt Reynolds will star instead).

Though it would be out of character for Beatty to agree to star for another director and/or producer at this stage of his career, the only thing certain about Beatty is that nothing is ever certain until it's a done thing. "I can't define myself," he insists when asked for insights into his challenging psyche. "My vision of life is constantly shifting. I tend to live day by day. Sometimes when you plan ahead, the future obliterates the present. That's why I never explain myself."

The future as Beatty currently contemplates it continues to revolve around the making of movies. Having made the grade as a producer, screenwriter, and director, he has modified his outlook on the movie business, no longer viewing it as an inconsequential preoccupation for an adult.

Like most of those the world considers workaholics, he sometimes dreams of escaping to a calmer, more peaceful existence. But the bottom line to his fantasies is that fantasies they will remain. Constantly striving, Beatty isn't one to stop and smell the roses unless he's timing himself with a stopwatch before getting back to work again.

"My idea of freedom and independence," he confessed not long ago, "is to live on top of a hill with clean air—no smog—and some good food vaguely in the area. The window is ajar, and there's a breeze that smells of geraniums or honeysuckle. And there's a room with a typewriter, where you go in for a few hours a day and tell your version of things. And you get a call from someone in a distant, dirty city who tells you that you can have more money and more time to write because people are so eager to read what you have to say. That's the fantasy of quitting. The other day I was thinking about quitting, and it was really attractive to me—for fifteen or twenty minutes.

"But then you go out to a movie theater and get this thrill when something good goes on the screen. And you want to raise your hand and say, 'Wait a minute, *wait a minute. I want to make one of those!'"*

He has made four of those thus far, and the thrill, though it's become more familiar, hasn't died; nor has the deeply rewarding satisfaction of a risk taken and a challenge met lost its savor. Instead of sitting back and packing it in, Beatty, as he approaches the half century mark, is pushing himself even harder to continue taking risks, to establish himself as an innovator who left his mark on motion pictures.

There are, of course, still worlds left for Beatty to conquer in the motion picture business. Though he modestly asserts he is more of a storyteller than a writer, he may write a screenplay solo someday, having trained by collaborating with one seasoned scriptwriter after another. Nor is it inconceivable that he might eventually be asked to take over as head of a studio, a job certain to appeal to him in terms of the power and control he could then assume. Or he may choose to try his hand at a film that's strictly documentary, an alternative to his fictionalizing biographical material. There are many paths he might choose within the film industry itself.

That he will stay in show business for some time to come is probable. Still a relatively young man, Beatty could make another four or five films even if he decides to change career in middle age. His selectivity as both an actor and a producer presents him with substantial blocks of time between commitments to counterbalance those periods when he spends twenty-four hours a day immersed in the project at hand.

During those "free" periods, Warren continues to pursue his two other great interests in life: politics and women. There's a distinct possibility that politics will one day edge out movies as his primary occupation. As for women, whatever the conflicts of his busy schedule, he has never failed to find time for romance. In dealing with the opposite sex, Beatty continues to act like the fictional character created by Rex Stout who ". . . was born with the attitude toward all attractive women that a fisherman has toward all the trout in the stream, and has never seen any reason to change it." For the time being, Warren remains the Compleat Angler.

20

WARREN BEATTY FOR PRESIDENT?

If and when the day comes that Warren turns his back on motion pictures completely, there's no doubt which field he would choose to embrace. He has long been drawn to the glamorous and powerful world of politics, and allurement enhanced by the theatrical aspects of compaigning. "The relationship between theater and politics fascinates me," he admits enthusiastically. "They both communicate ideas and both involve persuasion and compromise."

Were Warren to throw his hat into the ring and pursue a political office, those who know him best predict that, ambitious as he has always been, he would not be satisfied until he went straight to the top. In Leslie Caron's opinion, "If you woke him up in the middle of the night, before his defenses were up, if that is ever possible, and asked him what he wanted to be, I think he would say, 'President.' I don't think he'll stop until he's president."

Now that a former actor actually holds the highest office in America, the prospect of President Beatty isn't as far-fetched as it once would have been. But if that is Warren's fantasy, it's one he won't admit to. He says he's happy enough sticking to the campaign side of the game, arguing that though he's wise in the area of politics, he's ignorant when it comes to the administrative side of government.

"Politics is different from government," he explained in 1975. "I don't see government as something you can learn to do in a couple of weeks or months. I feel that part of the problem in this country is that we turn to people to administrate the government who aren't necessarily administrative personalities. The Senate isn't a place where one has the opportunity to exercise or develop his administrative capacities, but for the past twenty or thirty years, we've turned to senators for our presidential candidates.

"I wouldn't say that I'll never run for office," he added, leaving that important option open. "It's just that at this point there are other things I want to do. I'll probably make a few more movies."

Few may remember that Beatty almost "ran" for the Democratic presidential nomination in 1976. He wasn't seriously seeking the office of president, but considered offering himself as a "surrogate" candidate for a ticket of Hubert Humphrey for president and Edward Kennedy for vice president. Specifically, the actor was mulling over the possibility of putting his name on the ballot in the states of California, Ohio, and New Jersey.

Asked for his reasons by Christopher Lydon, reporting for *The New York Times*, Beatty explained, "I can see it as somewhat of an expression of resistance to the primary system itself, and as an expression of frustration at the fact that the leadership of the Democratic party—Kennedy, Humphrey, Muskie [Senator Edmund S. Muskie of Maine], McGovern, and others—are not participating in the primaries."

Beatty, who Lydon said was "taken seriously enough by Democratic professionals to have been courted by several of the active candidates, including Senator Henry M. Jackson of Washington and former Governor Jimmy Carter of Georgia," would not reveal who had proposed the idea that he put his name on the primary ballots. He also stressed that his move (which he ultimately did not make) would not have been a political ploy so much as an effort to clarify "the political aspects of the primary system itself," the new rules of which had, in his opinion, "made it virtually impossible for the office to seek the man."

Warren Beatty for president? He has intimated that any announcement of his personal political plans won't come until he is in his fifties. For the time being, he appears content to lend his support to full-time politicians and pick up what acumen he can under their leadership.

A new wrinkle in Warren's conflict between the public and the private man has recently developed, one that may thrust him into the political spotlight once again.

In an interview with United Press International late in 1982, former South Dakota Senator George McGovern revealed that he is again considering seeking the presidential nomination. Though he stated he would make no decision about the 1984 elections until "well into 1983," should he decide to run, he would most probably call upon Beatty for support.

If McGovern comes up with a viable solution—or promising suggestion—to cure America's economic woes, there's a good chance that Beatty would come out to help carry the banner for the Democratic candidate. And with support of the nuclear freeze so popular that Jonathan Schell's pro-freeze book, *The Fate of the Earth*, reached and maintained best-selling status, it is evident that McGovern would command respect as a candidate.

In 1975, when asked if he favored anyone on the political horizon, Beatty remarked, "There are a lot of men who would make good presidents, I think. But in this campaign it will be more difficult than ever for someone who's not widely known to come up on the Left, because the issue has changed from whether or not we should be in Vietnam to how are we going to solve our economic problems. The answer to the Vietnam question was quite clear by 1972, but the answer to our economic problems is not so clear, and certainly not clearly articulated by someone to whom the answer is clear. Consequently I think no one would be able to rally the support around his answer the way McGovern was able to rally support around his answer for Vietnam."

Several months after McGovern's announcement that he might choose to run, another longshot campaign for the Democratic nomination was announced as Beatty's friend and contemporary, forty-five-year-old Colorado Senator Gary Hart, tossed his hat into the ring.

This leaves Beatty with a choice of three close friends as Democratic hopefuls (Senator Cranston of California is also a contender) should he decide to actively campaign. All three trailed behind the front-runners—former Vice-President Walter Mondale and Senator John Glenn of Ohio—at the time Hart's candidacy was announced, so it came as no surprise that many newsworthy Democrats (Warren among them) remained mum on their favorite for the nomination. With so many runners in the race, the astute campaigner would be wise to wait until after the convention to press his support.

Would it be against Warren's interest to involve himself in a political campaign at this point? Not if he nurtures dreams of his own political career, since the campaign for a Democratic president in 1984 could provide an irrestible launching pad for his own political aspirations. On the other hand, if his chosen candidate should choose to run on a platform of economic belt-tightening, the active support of a man who blithely spent at least $33 million on a single motion picture might prove to be as much of a hindrance as a help.

And yet, in spite of his millionaire playboy image, Beatty also projects himself as an intelligent, concerned citizen with the kind of orderly mind that's a boon in governmental areas. One of the few movie stars—if not the only one—who has ever taken a correspondence course in Russian, he has also visited the Soviet Union enough times to speak knowledgeably on Soviet issues. A sophisticated thinker, he is well read and well informed while, unlike the late Adlai Stevenson, Warren manages to come across as a populist rather than an egghead.

A man who has never made a rash professional decision in his life, Beatty exudes caution and competence. He gives to his own thoughts the same threefold consideration he gave to the scripts he read as a young actor, scribbling what he calls "the crap" on white sheets of paper, then transferring it to pink bond as it's refined. Then, he says, "by the time it gets to yellow, it's an idea."

Warren also has the memory power of a born politician. He remembers telephone numbers for years, even if he never dialed them more than once or twice. He can recall every item on the menu at a dinner he shared with someone a decade ago. And, with a familiarity that's charming and never offensive, he'll speak to an acquaintance he hasn't seen for years with the same easy camaraderie as if he'd been with him the previous night. These are all positive characteristics for a politician, as is Beatty's habit of looking the other person straight in the eyes during a conversation. ("I study eyes for a clue to truth," he once stated.)

Added to all these other qualities is the fact that Beatty just plain looks more serious these days. Middle age has softened the once arrogant face without leaving it any less handsome. The network of lines around the myopic blue eyes, the more frequently worn glasses, the cleanly shorn chestnut hair, and conservative Glen plaid and pin-striped suits all contribute to the portrait of a man who scorns frivolity. And, as Beatty himself predicted, the nation has gradually grown less concerned with the private lives of politicans. The revelations of JFK's extracurricular activities while in office no longer raise many eyebrows; not even the Far Right, which supported Ronald Reagan so doggedly, was unfavorably swayed by Nancy Davis Reagan's being his second wife, Reagan having married and divorced Jane Wyman back when both were major screen stars.

Most important, Beatty has proven himself to be a man who, in spite of the various derogatory remarks he's made about the press, has learned to manipulate the media for his own benefit and who has nurtured a self-image that's as enticing as it is paradoxical. He is a legend, and the accoutrements of that legend are not discrepant with the stuff of successful politicians. He's a self-made man, an unobtrusive millionaire, a grass roots humanist, an astute businessman, a modest genius, a diligent worker. He is instantly recognizable to the American public, an important factor in the search for political office, often outweighing any ill effects of negative publicity.

The fact that people are preconditioned to view him a certain way because of what they've read may have its drawbacks, but, as Beatty asserts, ". . . there's a positive side, too. When you meet someone, you're not a total stranger to them, and sometimes that can facilitate things; at least you can start by correcting wrong impressions. I wouldn't relate this strictly to women, either. . . ." Easily recognizable—Beatty is one of those stars who could never blend into the woodwork; even if spotted on a casual stroll, he is every inch the movie star—Warren has cleverly refused to let himself be overpromoted. He is not a familiar face on talk shows; he does not play the Hollywood game show circuit; he cautiously rations the number of interviews he will grant even to promote his own productions. A celebrity whose detachment has preserved his Olympian stature, Beatty in person remains a great draw.

In any case, Warren's political bent should never be taken lightly. Doubtless, his political activity will continue to occupy him in the years to come, and it's likely that it will one day take precedence over everything else in his life. Considering the seriousness of his political intentions, it's hardly surprising that the latest woman in his life is one prominent on the fringes of the political arena. Considering Warren Beatty's record, it's even less surprising that she's a well-known celebrity.

21

THE REAL
WARREN BEATTY

Like Warren, Jessica Savitch is often described as "a work-aholic," "driven," and "a perfectionist." In 1977, Savitch, then not yet thirty, was plucked from relative obscurity as an anchorwoman at KYW-TV in Philadelphia and thrust into the spotlight of the national "NBC Nightly News" as their Washington correspondent. By 1980, she was covering the presidential race; by 1982, she was so famous that her autobiography was published.

Though she dislikes being singled out for her driving ambition, even Savitch won't deny that her steady climb to the top has been exhausting. "I've called a moratorium on goals," she announced in 1979. "When you constantly set new goals, life can go by too fast. Now I just want to grow in the job that I have."

It's not an easy job, requiring the slender blonde (at five foot five, she wears a size 3 dress) to commute weekly between Washington and New York in her job as anchorwoman and Washington correspondent.

Also like Beatty, Jessica has long despaired over being considered no more than a pretty face. In a talk with Peter Ross Range for *TV Guide*, she lamented, "No matter what I do, no matter how many awards I get for reporting, people will always say that I am 'Jessica Savitch, the petite blonde,' not 'the award-winning reporter.' I've decided I'm not going to apologize for my looks anymore. This is it. This is how I look."

Jessica, who grew up in Margate, New Jersey, near Atlantic City, decided while still in her teens that she wanted to be an announcer. At Ithaca College, she worked part-time as a model and was already on the radio, as a disc jockey in Rochester, New York.

The first job that made any difference in her career was at KHOU-TV in Houston, where she went from a staff position to being the first female anchor in Texas TV history in just ten months. Shortly after her promotion, she was offered the post in Philadelphia, where, according to a friend, "the job became her whole life."

From the start of her professional career, Savitch pursued her climb to the top with a single-mindedness not unlike the young Warren Beatty's. Whereas many on-camera newsmen depend on others to write their copy, Jessica has always written and covered her own stories. She was equally attentive when it came to developing the kind of image she wanted to have, borrowing clothes from Blum's department store where her good friend Rita Rappaport worked, then returning them after the newscast. She also commuted regularly to New York so she could study voice with coach Lilyan Wilder. And she still found time to ski, jog, and play tennis.

Like Beatty, Savitch embraces challenges. She's determined to have it all.

Unlike Beatty, having it all for Savitch has meant marriage as well as a career, though she's been tragically unlucky on this score. Her first marriage ended in divorce; her second husband, gynecologist Donald Payne, committed suicide not long after Jessica suffered a miscarriage in 1981.

In spring of 1982, Savitch, recovering from surgery and wishing to put the finishing touches on her book, accepted an invitation to spend a month with her friends Rita and Sam Rappaport at their house in Puerto Rico. She had already turned down an invitation from another source—saying no when Warren Beatty first asked her out. This wasn't because she was unexcited (according to Mrs. Rappaport, Jessica called her and exclaimed, "Guess who asked me for a date!"), but because of scheduling conflicts and because the newswoman was embarrassed to tell Beatty she hadn't seen *Reds*.

In Puerto Rico, Jessica and Rita Rappaport saw the movie, and when they returned to the mainland, Jessica accepted Warren's next invitation, telling her friend afterward that she'd found Beatty down-to-earth.

Savitch herself has been close-mouthed to fellow members of the media about her relationship with the star, the first celebrity with whom she's been involved.

Savitch would appear to fulfill any requirements Beatty has where the opposite sex is concerned. She's well known in her own right, beautiful, and politically au courant. And, perhaps more than any woman with whom he's been linked, Jessica can relate to Beatty's unquenched thirst for success.

"There has not been a single moment in my career when I didn't say, 'Is this all there is?'" Savitch reflected in a candid moment. "Yep, this is all there is. Nothing is all you think it will be. But it really ain't so bad, is it?

"The problem is that whenever you think of succeeding, you think you'll be happy. You think 'happiness' will be written on the ticket. It's not. Success does not have to bring happiness. Success brings success. I think I succeeded because so many people told me I couldn't."

Like Beatty when he decided to produce *Bonnie and Clyde*, Savitch was determined to show the "big boys" she could make it on their terms. And like Beatty, her success has not made her indolent. She lives from achievement to achievement. During her "moratorium on goals," she relaxed by writing *Anchorwoman*, her autobiography.

Will Jessica Savitch be the woman to end up as Mrs. Warren Beatty? She'd certainly be a proper politician's wife, having all the credentials for the role. And in today's loosening morality, her divorce would not be a major factor in a husband's campaign. The only consideration in doubt is whether Savitch would be content with the role of helpmate; she's more likely the type to run for office herself.

In 1974, Beatty confessed that he was "too dependent" on love. In the past, he said, he had handled that aspect of his makeup by not getting involved. Now he just approached the opposite sex with more caution.

This same caution led him—during the filming of *Reds*—to open several large accounts in Swiss banks. As he explained it, "I'm putting my money as far away from Hollywood as possible, because [of] all those new laws about having to pay half your assets to a woman you've been in a romantic relationship with.

"I've had many genuinely serious relationships with women . . . and we've lived together without getting married. When it was over, it was over and that was that. . . .

"From now on, if any former lady love wants to find my money, she'll have to search all over the Swiss Alps to get it."

In these days of palimony, Warren isn't unique among bachelors in his wariness. But, cautious and suspicious though he may be, he still admits that he sharply feels the lack of a serious relationship, a commitment, in his life.

Speaking with Alan Ebert in 1976, Beatty admitted, "It is very important to me. I *need* to be with someone I know well, who knows me well. It is very lonely for me to live without a woman, without relating life with or to another person. Somehow, when you are *with* someone, it is like seeing life through four eyes rather than through two. It's a big cliché, but it is also a big truth: Life means so much more when it is shared."

It is to Beatty's credit that his words don't have the ring of hypocrisy. He has seemed to be happiest, most content, when there has been one special woman in his life, be it Joan Collins, Natalie Wood, Leslie Caron, Julie Christie, Michelle Phillips, or Diane Keaton. Love is the humanizing force, and Warren, who has always existed on a rather lofty cerebral level, seems to realize better than anyone else his need for a woman to keep him in touch with basic human feelings.

As he grows older, Beatty admits he is more drawn toward, if not the monogamous ideal, some sort of relationship that will bring him fulfillment and permanence. He has learned firsthand the value of compromise on the political scene; he seems to be accepting the inevitability of compromise on the domestic front as well.

At forty-six, Warren Beatty is a man who has lived to see his boyhood dreams come true. As a producer, he is respected and sought after, a creator of drama, a manipulator of men, someone who is "bankable" in every sense of the word. He is fabulously wealthy, and his wealth has taught him that, after a certain bank balance is reached, money "ceases to be a remedy for much."

Warren Beatty for president? Perhaps that remains the ultimate challenge, the last battlefield for a man who achieves one ambition only to replace it with the next. Then again, perhaps the ultimate challenge is something simpler, more mundane, something no more exotic than the mere legal connection of a man and a woman by a paper certificate.

Beatty the romantic likes to gaze at the stars through the telescope in his Mulholland Drive home, sends women flowers, leaves messages full of whimsy on his friends' answering machines. Beatty the romantic had Bonnie and Clyde longing for a "normal" life together, George the hairdresser aging overnight from lack of love, Louise Bryant gazing wistfully at a child but pregnant only with the bitter knowledge that she and Reed would never have one. Beatty the pragmatist is a wheeler and dealer in the best Hollywood boardroom style, a man for whom the telephone is an extra appendage, a producer whose dreams translate into dollars and cents, a sly political campaigner, a lone wolf who changes women as blithely as he checks in and out of hotels.

Both Beattys are the real Warren Beatty. It remains to be seen whether he will someday effect a lasting, and satisfying, balance between the two. And in the long run, that's the most intricate challenge of them all.

Index